HAUNTED PLYMOUTH

Merchant's House, Plymouth.

HAUNTED PLYMOUTH

Kevin Hynes

Dedicated to the memory of
John Charles Hallybone (1949–2009)

First published 2010
Reprinted 2012

The History Press
The Mill, Brimscombe Port
Stroud, Gloucestershire, GL5 2QG
www.thehistorypress.co.uk

British Library Cataloguing in Publication Data.
A catalogue record for this book is available from the British Library.

ISBN 978 0 7524 5232 6
Typesetting and origination by The History Press
Printed in Great Britain

Contents

'All that we see or seem is but a dream within a dream.'

Edgar Allan Poe

Derry's Clock Tower and the old Plymouth Theatre Royal. (Courtesy of Derek Tait)

About the Author

Kevin Hynes was born and brought up in Plymouth. His interest in ghosts and the supernatural stretches back to his early childhood. For the past ten years Kevin has been actively investigating the paranormal, which includes spending time at a wide array of haunted locations throughout the UK. Previously he has been involved with several paranormal groups, contributing to the running of charity nights and ghost walks, and has appeared on local television and radio in relation to his work.

He co-founded Supernatural Investigations (UK) with the aim of conducting serious paranormal research. Kevin also founded Haunted Plymouth, which specialises in Plymouth ghost walks.

www.supernaturalinvestigations.org.uk
www.hauntedplymouth.com

Kevin Hynes on Plymouth Hoe, 2010.

Introduction & Acknowledgements

Plymouth is a city rich in history, atmosphere and its fair share of ghosts, ghouls and hauntings. Much like the Pilgrim Fathers who set sail from Plymouth in 1620, *Haunted Plymouth* embarks upon a paranormal voyage that will help you to discover why this ancient port has such a wide variety of supernatural phenomena.

In researching this book I have uncovered a wealth of paranormal history associated with the city. Drawing on historical and contemporary sources, the book features both old and new ghost stories, as well as exclusive interviews with eyewitnesses and previously unpublished investigation accounts carried out by the author and the Supernatural Investigation (UK) team.

I would like to thank the following people for their assistance and help with the compilation of this book. My appreciation and special thanks must go to my colleagues in Supernatural Investigations (UK): Stuart and Becky Andrews, Clare Buckland, Jason Higgs, David Hallybone, and Damian and Francesca Haydon for all their contributions, time and effort, not to mention the countless paranormal investigations we have undertaken together as an active investigation group. It has been an inspirational and enjoyable journey.

Thanks to Byron Jackson, founder of Haunted Devon (www.haunted-devon.co.uk); Derek Tait for his assistance with the photographs; Patricia Duff from Heart FM; Amanda Percival, owner of Shirley Valentine's; Jenny Allen, my sister; Liz Thurkettle, friend and fellow Supernatural Investigation (UK) investigator; Rose MacInnes from Black Friars Distillery; Rob from Chris Robinson's Gallery on New Street; The Tudor Rose Tea Room on New Street; Duncan Jago at Reel Cinema Plymouth; Diane, owner of Poppy's Guest House; Vicky Pope at Boringdon Hall; and the many more individuals who have given me their time and ghostly stories.

Above all, I would like to thank my parents, Viv and Des Hynes, my wife Gina and my two fantastic children, Sean and Chloe, for their patience and understanding with regard to my passion for the paranormal. Also to all my family and friends – you know who you are.

All photographs in this publication, unless otherwise stated, are copyright of the author. I have made every effort to contact copyright holders and gain permission for the use of any copyright material, but apologise if I have inadvertently missed anyone out.

Kevin Hynes, 2010

one

The Historic Barbican

The Elizabethan House

In the late fifteenth century, Plymouth was a prosperous, bustling port due to an influx of ships and crew, not to mention privateers, craftsmen and merchants who flocked to the seaport. The need for new housing was imperative; this led to the development of New Street. A number of the properties were purposely built for the likes of sea merchants and sea captains, who relied upon the proximity of the sea for their livelihood.

The Elizabethan House on the Barbican dates from 1584 and is a restored captain's dwelling now open to the public. Even today it is not hard to imagine the likes of Sir Walter Raleigh, Sir Francis Drake or Captain Cook strolling down the narrow cobbled streets which line the Barbican.

The most well-known story is from an archaeologist at the Plymouth Museum who had an unexpected experience on a very cold, dank October evening in 1983. The gentleman had arrived early to prepare for the evening's lecture. It was around dusk when he first entered the Elizabethan House and made his way up the old winding staircase. As he ascended the stairs he heard a most peculiar sound, so he hurried to find out where this strange noise was emanating from. As he entered one of the upper floor rooms he saw, to his amazement, a small wooden child's cradle rocking from side to side all by itself, as if some invisible hand was rocking the cradle at a steady pace. At this point the archaeologist turned heel and hurried back down the winding staircase,

The Elizabethan House, New Street.

feeling quite unnerved by what he had seen. By now a number of guests had started to arrive, and he felt compelled to inform them of what, only moments earlier, he had just witnessed up on the upper levels of the Elizabethan House. He even managed to convince a number to join him upstairs to see if the child's cradle would again move freely of its own accord. So, once again, the lecturer ascended the wooden stairs, followed by a handful of his guests. They entered the room and stood around the child's cradle. At this point the cradle was stationary and everyone talked amongst themselves, joking about the situation, but the laughter was cut short as the cradle did indeed start to rock once again from left to right.

Local legend states that the ghost of an infant child has been seen within this small wooden cradle. This has been witnessed only for a brief moment and then the apparition suddenly vanishes.

The figure of a young girl aged around eight has been seen sitting in the corner of the first-floor room. A number of people have seen her looking out of the window

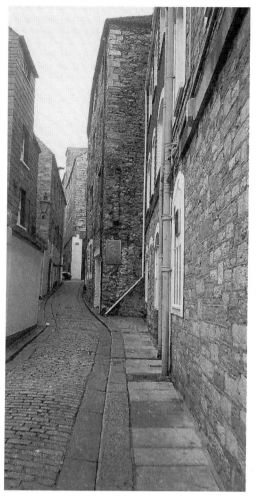

Cobbled streets in the Barbican, full of history, legend and tradition.

The wooden infants' cradle in the Elizabethan House.

Early photograph of the wooden cradle. (Courtesy of Derek Tait)

The window from which the phantom girl has been sighted.

whilst they have been walking around the upper floor of this building, and passers-by in the street have been drawn to look up at this window. On a number of occasions passers-by have caught a glimpse of this child looking back at them.

Furniture in the Elizabethan House.

There are many reports of cold spots within the Elizabethan House, and even on a very hot summer's day it is claimed that certain areas become icy cold, even if only for a brief moment.

Certain members of staff have commented that while on the ground floor, they have heard items of furniture being dragged around the upper levels, although upon inspection nothing is reported to be out of place.

Number 34 New Street

Just a short distance from the Elizabethan House is No. 34 New Street; this quaint and attractive building is home to Chris Robinson's Gallery. I have visited this location on numerous occasions and, being a keen local historian, find the collection of books, photographs and pictures that are sold at these premises absolutely fascinating.

On one of my visits I had a very intriguing conversation with a gentleman named Rob, who has worked at the gallery for the past twenty years. Our conversation turned towards the supernatural and it was at this point that I enquired if Rob had ever encountered anything of a spooky nature himself whilst working at this fascinating location. He recalled to me a couple of events that he could not explain, beginning with an unnerving experience that occurred almost twenty years previously.

It was around eleven in the evening and Rob had decided to stay late to finish off some stencil work he had begun earlier in the day. He was working on the first floor of the building and the gallery had been closed for a number of hours. No one else was in

New Street, Barbican, c. 1890.
(Courtesy of John Van der Kiste)

the building at this time and everything on the ground floor was locked up and secure. All was quiet until the silence was suddenly broken by the sound of heavy footsteps running at pace down the old spiral staircase. Rob stated that the sound gave him a bit of a fright and recalled that the noise was so deafening that it sounded like a rugby player running down the stairs; he could even feel the vibration underfoot. Rob immediately jumped up and gave chase, running down the wooden staircase after the 'intruder'. By the time he entered the gallery and through to the main building entrance there was no sign of anyone; the door was still securely locked and there was no evidence that anyone had entered, or left, the building. Rob then carried out a thorough search of the entire building, even checking the cellar area. There was no rational explanation for who or what had been responsible for the thundering footsteps, and racing down the staircasewould have been quite a task as you really have to take your time manoeuvring up or down them.

Above: *Chris Robinson's Gallery at No. 34 New Street.*

Left: *A view along New Street.*

A couple of years after this event Rob received a visit from a lady, who told him that she had lived in the property many years before it became a shop. She enquired if it was OK to have a look around the building, to rekindle some old memories; Rob was more than happy for her to do so. The lady then asked if Sambo was still around. Rob explained that he had been working there for a number of years and was not aware of anyone called Sambo – to which the lady replied that Sambo was not a person, but a ghost. Rob immediately remembered the experience he had had a number of years previously, but before he retold his own experience he asked the lady who Sambo was and how she knew that he was indeed a ghost. The woman told Rob that she had experienced some very odd things whilst living at No. 34 New Street and none more so than the sound of someone running down the old spiral staircase, even though at the time no one else was in the dwelling. The lady called upon a friend who was a sensitive and, as she walked around the building, she immediately picked up on a young boy named Sambo, who had apparently been murdered. It was Sambo who was responsible for the loud footsteps running down the stairs. Rob was at this point amazed at the similarity between the previous owner's account and his own experience within the ancient walls of No. 34 New Street. The meeting of Rob and the lady gives this ghostly tale a great deal of credibility, as two independent witnesses encountered the same haunting.

As an aside, whenever Rob's daughter came to visit him at the gallery, there was one room on the upper floor that she would not enter, as it had such an ominous and sinister feel to it. One wonders if she was picking up on the past impressions left behind by previous souls that resided at No. 34 New Street?

Shirley Valentine's Taverna

Located in New Street on the Barbican, this Elizabethan building has been used for a number of different purposes. In more recent times it was known as the Robin Hood Club, while in 1823 it was the Robin Hood Inn. Today it is home to Shirley Valentine's Taverna, which serves a delicious range of mouth-watering Greek and Turkish cuisine.

Amanda Percival is the current owner of Shirley Valentine's Taverna. I have recently been in communication with her after making her acquaintance on one of my Plymouth ghost walks. Amanda told me that she has experienced some ghostly goings-on since she took over the lease on the property in 2008, and the following is a brief description of the things that have been witnessed by herself and others at the taverna:

When we first took over the lease on the property in 2008 we undertook a few decorating / refurbishment jobs. Sometimes I would be there on my own decorating and I would get the impression and feeling of someone being in the room with me or coming up the stairs. I have heard footsteps on a number of occasions.

Since we have been open and trading, both myself and other staff members have heard footsteps or movement on the first floor and both sets of staircases. I have caught a glimpse of a person's outline and just the top of someone's head going down the stairs. A member of staff has experienced items falling off a window sill and landing unnaturally when no one has been close to the window, which was also closed at the time. We did not feel frightened or threatened, just intrigued.

The activity at Shirley Valentine's continues today – and most recently the apparition of a woman has been seen standing in one particular section of the upstairs eating area.

Shirley Valentine's Taverna, New Street.

Above: *Shirley Valentine's restaurant area.*

Left: *The corner where the spectre has been seen in Shirley Valentine's.*

Tudor Rose Tea Room

The Tudor Rose Tea Room in New Street is an ancient property which boasts an array of imposing spirits.

On a recent visit to this elegant Tea Room I asked a member of staff if she had ever encountered anything out of the ordinary whilst working there. She replied that over the past few years there has been a wide range of paranormal activity, for instance, sightings of figures in the Tea Rooms and ponderous footsteps have been heard above on the first floor, even though at the time no one was in the vicinity. She then went on to explain that items have been moved around the kitchen area – classic poltergeist activity – and that one customer who ordered a cake to go with his tea was left horror-stricken as he witnessed the cake fly off the counter. It was as if it had been pushed by some invisible force – bringing a whole new meaning to the term fast food!

An unnerving encounter was experienced first hand by an acquaintance of mine. In 2008 Diane decided to visit the Tudor Rose Tea Room with her son. They ordered and paid for their drinks and sat quietly in the larger of the two rooms. After a short time Diane's attention was drawn towards an elderly lady sitting in the far corner of the room, who, for some reason, kept looking over at Diane and her son. The woman then spoke to Diane, saying, 'This is my house and I am gentry.' Diane smiled, then looked away and continued to sip her tea. She looked up again to see if the elderly woman was still gazing across at her, but was mystified to see that she had completely vanished! This was most peculiar as there was no physical way that the woman could have left the room without being noticed, plus she would have had to walk past Diane and her son and exited through a glass-panelled door to leave the vicinity. It was only at this point that Diane realised how elegantly dressed the woman had been. This elderly, well-dressed apparition has been witnessed many times since. What I find most amazing is that this phantom actually spoke to Diane, implying that this is an intelligent spirit quite happy to communicate directly with the living.

New Street.

Black Friars Distillery

Black Friars Distillery on the Barbican is the oldest working gin distillery in England: world-famous Plymouth Gin has been produced here since 1793.

The building dates as far back as the early fourteenth century; the most intact part of the building is the refectory room, which was once a medieval hall and has a hull-shaped timber roof, built in 1431, thus making this building one of the oldest in Plymouth. The distillery was formerly a monastery inhabited by the Black Friars, from whom the distillery gained its name. Other uses for this building have included it being a debtors' prison. It is also believed that a number of the Pilgrim Fathers spent their last night here in 1620, before making the short walk down to the harbour to set sail for their epic voyage to America.

Black Friars Distillery, Southside Street.

Workers in days gone by at Black Friars Distillery. (Courtesy of Derek Tait)

A number of spirits reside within the old stone walls of the distillery – and I am not just talking about those in the bottles! In more recent times, a number of all-night paranormal investigations have taken place at the distillery and a number of presences have been seen and picked up on by psychics.

I would like to offer my personal thanks to Byron Jackson, the founder of the paranormal group, Haunted Devon, for giving me permission to include part of their investigation report. Haunted Devon investigated the Black Friars Distillery in 2006 and the quotes refer to their psychic medium's findings:

Black Friars Distillery – the home of Plymouth Gin. (Courtesy of Derek Tait)

Still Room
† The psychic medium sensed that a man had fallen from the still
† A woman in her twenties, believed to be a prostitute, enters the building from the rear of the location, which is known as Black Friars Lane. She is accompanied by a young boy aged around 7 or 8. The boy is related to the young woman but he is not her son
† A past explosion was sensed, which left a man with burns
† American soldiers from the time of the Second World War were sensed in this area. The medium felt that they were carrying boxes

Cellar Area
† The medium sensed that this was once a long tunnel leading from the street through to the lane behind the distillery. In the 1700s it was sensed that paupers would have rested and slept in this area at night
† A strong smell of sack cloth was picked up here. Sanitary conditions were poor, leading to many deaths. The deceased 'were simply put on the road, only to disappear before dawn'
† The psychic felt that this area was used as an air-raid shelter during the Second World War
† Overall, the medium picked up on a vast amount of residual energy

Stock Room
† One of Haunted Devon's psychics sensed that a number of murders dating back over a long period of time had taken place in this area

† This spot was felt to have once been used by paupers. Death seemed quite apparent in this area

Ladies' Restroom
The following are direct quotes from the Haunted Devon investigation report, referring to what the psychic medium sensed in this part of the building:

> A lady with two children hides from someone here. They were destitute but afraid of something or someone following them, but could not say what.

> A World War Two lady was stabbed here. The gasp sensation reflects where the knife penetrated her. Her death was a result of an argument over personal belongings in the shelter [a small rectangular box]. Her assailant was another woman, who was in uniform and wearing long green socks. The victim was younger [18 or 19 years]. The murderer was older. The whole issue was covered up and forgotten given the circumstances of the time. The victim had few / no relatives so she was easy to dispose of. There were threats to keep quiet about it or access would be denied to the shelter.

Street Area (located just inside the entrance to Black Friars Distillery)

> There is a lower area underground – or lower than it is today. This was used to hold people but much of this was not legally binding. People were put in here if they owed money or rent. The conditions were terrible and the area was divided up, possibly into cells. [This was the site of the debtors' prison.]

On a historical note, during the Second World War part of Black Friars Distillery was hit by a German fire bomb. The distillery offices and many of the records were destroyed, which left the production crippled by ingredients rationing at this time.

I have had the pleasure of being given a guided tour by Rose, a member of staff at the Black Friars Distillery. While on my brief visit I asked Rose about the paranormal activity which has been witnessed here over the years. Rose mentioned a few of the presences that have been encountered, confirming what the paranormal group Haunted Devon had previously picked up during their time spent at this ancient location. The most commonly witnessed ghost is that of a young girl named Lucy, who is believed to roam around the whole building. The ghost of a man named Charles is said to haunt the Still Room, and a young prostitute named Elizabeth has appeared in the past. I have also been informed that a monk-like figure has been sighted in certain parts of the ancient building.

Mediums have sensed a tragic past event that occurred in the area that is today the ladies' restroom. It is believed that a lost female soul haunts this area; she met her demise after being brutally stabbed to death upon this spot. Today, a number of women who visit the toilets claim to be overcome with dread; not many hang around to find out why there is such an oppressive feeling in this part of the building.

This location features in my Haunted Plymouth ghost walk, and in the past a number of the female ghost walk participants have commented on the ladies' restroom and stated

Workers at Black Friars Distillery.
(Courtesy of Derek Tait)

Workers at Black
Friars Distillery.
(Courtesy of Derek
Tait)

that the atmosphere in this area feels very oppressive. One woman actually stated that she would never return there as it felt so negative.

At the time of writing, I am in talks with Black Friars Distillery to undertake an all-night paranormal investigation with Supernatural Investigations (UK) at this historic venue.

The Cooperage

The Cooperage Inn is located on Vauxhall Street, a stone's throw from Plymouth's historic Barbican. The apparition of a lady dressed in black with a large black bonnet is said to occupy this old drinking house. She is believed to originate from the Crimean War era and has spooked many staff and visitors over the years.

A woman who once worked at the old inn claims that the ghost has made herself known to her a number of times. She recalled that on one occasion she was carrying out her duties on the ground floor of the building after closing time, at around 3 o'clock in the morning, when she heard a noise coming from behind the bar. Believing it to be the club owner, whom, moments earlier, she had seen from the corner of her eye walk into the bar area, she did not turn to look up but merely went about her business.

The woman decided to strike up a conversation with the club owner, telling him what stock was required from the cash and carry, but after a few moments she felt slightly miffed when she received no response.

At this point she heard the owner walk around the front of the bar towards her, and, without looking up, she asked, 'Are you ignoring me?' to which there was no reply.

The woman looked up, expecting to see her boss, but instead she came face-to-face with the Lady in Black, standing no more than a couple of feet in front of her. In that brief moment, which seemed to last an eternity, the shade turned to her right and walked past the staff member towards a big wooden door, which used to lead to the old loading bay. Just before she reached the door, the staff member called out and went to confront the strange woman, who was in the building past closing time. But before she even had a chance to stop and question the woman, the Lady in Black vanished into thin air, right in front of her eyes. The staff member was amazed, as the woman had been so clear and lifelike. At this point her boss walked into the bar area and asked who she had been talking to. On telling him of her encounter, the club owner calmly told her that he too had seen this phantom woman – on a number of occasions!

One evening, as I was leading a group on my Plymouth ghost walk, I stopped opposite the Cooperage as per usual and retold the above account. A number of the guests on the tour decided to take some photographs of this ancient drinking house.

After I had completed the tale of the 'Lady in Black', we were joined by a smartly-dressed gentleman, who kindly asked why people were taking photographs of his inn, so I explained.

The gentleman, who was intrigued, told me that he had only recently purchased the Cooperage and had already experienced, along with several of his staff, some unusual events, including objects that had been placed in one spot then mysteriously turning up in a completely different area. He also told me that a large, dark figure had been seen by himself and a number of his staff. On further investigation, no one was found on the premises who matched the description.

The Minerva Inn

The Minerva Inn in Looe Street was built around 1540, which makes it one of Plymouth's oldest drinking houses. A plaque on a building just up from the Minerva Inn indicates

The Minerva Inn, Looe Street.

that local hero Sir Francis Drake once resided here, and I am quietly confident that Drake would have enjoyed a few flagons of ale at this very inn.

There is quite a bit of history attached to the inn in regards to press gangs, which operated heavily in this particular area in the eighteenth century. It is believed that some of the Minerva's clients would have been beaten, before being forcibly led through a tunnel located inside the Minerva to the Parade area of the Barbican. The unfortunate victim would awake with a headache, only to realise he was on board a man of war ship. The entrance to the tunnel can still be found in the Minerva today. This tunnel would almost certainly have also served its purpose for smugglers, as smuggling was a major part of everyday life in times gone by.

I would like to offer my thanks once again to Byron Jackson, the founder of the paranormal group Haunted Devon (www.haunted-devon.co.uk), for giving me permission to include information gathered by his psychic mediums during a paranormal investigation that took place at the Minerva Inn in 2006.

As you have read, the Minerva has had a long and colourful history and it is of no surprise that a number of its past visitors still frequent this ancient inn, including no fewer than five phantom prostitutes and the shade of a young girl wearing a Victorian-style dress. An Elizabethan lady has also appeared to a number of individuals; it is believed that she may have been one of the inn's old barmaids.

A menacing, angry phantom has also been sighted at the Minerva Inn. Those unfortunate enough to come face-to-face with this restless spirit are left feeling slightly shocked and baffled, for when this apparition appears all he proceeds to do is scream at them. Who is this man? What is the reason for his ghostly wail? Could he have been a victim of the press gangs, or is there another reason why he is unable to rest in peace?

two

The City

Foot Anstey Solicitors, Derry's Cross

Foot Anstey Solicitors is situated at Derry's Cross close to Derry's Clock Tower, which is aptly named after William Derry, a former Mayor of Plymouth. The solicitors' building was formerly home to Westward TV and, later, Television South West (TSW); some of you may recall the likes of Gus Hunnybun.

It is believed that this building was built upon the site of an old Plymouth Westwell Cemetery and is therefore believed to be where a number of Plymothians were laid to rest, not to mention a number of French Napoleonic prisoners of war. It is said that the bodies of these Napoleonic soldiers were moved to another Plymouth graveyard during the building's construction and it is their ghosts that haunt the studios.

The night watchman for TSW at the time had heard stories relating to one of the large studios being haunted, but he took these with a pinch of salt. However, his blasé attitude was short-lived, for he himself had a close encounter of the paranormal kind in the early hours whilst carrying out his rounds with his trusty torch.

He was in a particularly dark area of the studio, where it was so deadly quiet you could hear a pin drop, when, suddenly, the atmosphere became icy cold and, out of the darkness,

 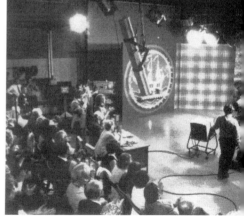

Westward TV studios in the 1970s. (Courtesy of Derek Tait)

he heard sinister laughter, followed by a male voice speaking fluent French. Suffice to say he did not hang around for long.

The Grand Hotel

The world-famous Grand Hotel is situated upon the historic Plymouth Hoe, and was once known as Plymouth's flagship hotel. The seventy-seven bedroom, grade II listed hotel boasted some of the finest sea views in all of Europe. It was designed and built by John Pethick in 1879, who was also responsible for the construction of The Duke of Cornwall Hotel located close by.

Shortly after the completion of The Grand a tragic accident occurred, which evolved into a classic haunting.

Legend states that two men were the catalyst for the spine-chilling phantom that haunts The Grand. An Italian and a Spaniard were involved in a fight over a beautiful young woman on the fourth floor of this Victorian building. During the scuffle, the woman in question intervened and tried to put a stop to the fight. Unfortunately, one of the men accidentally knocked her over the banisters, and she fell to her death. Since this tragic event, the apparition of a young woman in a Victorian dress has been witnessed gliding silently along the corridor on the fourth floor.

On 7 September 2003, emergency crews from Devon and Cornwall were called to The Grand to tackle a fire caused by an electrical fault. The fire raged through the building, gutting the entire upper floor and destroying the roof, forcing the hotel's closure. Fortunately no one was killed or injured during the blaze, although it took over a hundred fireman and twelve appliances to bring the fire under control.

At the time of writing, developers have decided to rebuild The Grand Hotel as luxury apartments, although I have been told by a reliable source that as work continues paranormal activity has increased.

Plymouth Hoe, with the Grand Hotel in the distance. (Courtesy of Derek Tait)

Number 10-13 Lockyer Street

This building was acquired in 1887 by the Young Women's Christian Association (YWCA), at which time it was used as a hostel for young women travelling to London and other cities throughout England looking to start work.

The building was destroyed during air raids on 20 March 1941. It took twelve years to rebuild and was re-opened by Queen Elizabeth the Queen Mother in March 1953.

During the bombing, the main air-raid shelter situated in Lockyer Street took a direct hit, killing a mother and her three children. Some time later the YWCA hostel was also hit during an air raid: five female members of staff, three male residents and three female visitors were killed during the blast. It is said that the basement of this building was used as a makeshift morgue for the bodies.

The building today is owned by Westcountry Housing Association, who still use this building as a hostel. On many occasions staff and residents have commented on a feeling of being watched, or even followed, only to find that no one is present at the time.

One member of staff recalls her first day at work in the building; she was working as a secretary in the office and was alone. A lady in a 1940s-style dress entered the room and began her cleaning duties. She had with her an old vacuum cleaner, which she plugged into the socket on the wall, and proceeded to clean.

The new member of staff said hello, but the cleaner did not seem to notice her and carried on with her work. Feeling slightly uncomfortable, the secretary decided to leave the room and allow the woman to continue to clean. While out of the office, the secretary

An early photograph of Lockyer Street. (Courtesy of Derek Tait)

inquired with another member of staff what the cleaner's name was, only to be told that no one of this description was on the staff team. Not only this, but the cleaner had finished work hours previously. On returning to the office there was indeed no sign of the female cleaner. Convinced she had not imagined what she had seen, the secretary looked towards the wall where she had witnessed the woman plug her vacuum into the socket. But to her amazement there was no sign of the electrical socket. Could this ghost have been a former staff member going about her daily cleaning duties?

The Octagon

The Octagon is situated just off Plymouth's Union Street. It was here, during the aftermath of a devastating air raid over Plymouth in the Second World War, that two young children had an encounter with a spectre. A ten-year-old girl, accompanied by her eight-year-old brother, walked amongst the rubble in search of the missing family cat. While they searched for their beloved feline, a woman joined them and began to search alongside the two children. A few moments went by when, all of a sudden, the woman lost her footing and began to stumble on the small mountain of rubble. Instinctively, one of the children went to grab her hand to offer assistance, but she completely vanished before the children's very eyes. It was not until the shocked children returned to their family and told their odd experience that they realised the woman had never once spoken to either of them whilst assisting in the search for the family cat.

The Old Treasury

Today, the Old Treasury is a pleasant restaurant and wine bar, but in the past the building was used, amongst other things, as a workhouse, the old Plymouth Treasury and a police station. This building is apparently built upon the site of an old French prisoner of war graveyard. Vivid sightings of full-blown apparitions have been witnessed within these old granite walls.

Reel Cinema

The Reel Cinema, previously known as the ABC cinema, is situated at Derry's Cross. On 11 April 1937, Plymouth's old Theatre Royal was demolished to make way for a more modern cinema and in its place rose the Royal Cinema, owned by the Associated British Cinemas (ABC). The cinema opened on 15 July 1938 and was one of only a handful of buildings to survive the Plymouth Blitz during the Second World War. The world-famous Liverpudlian band The Beatles performed on stage at the ABC on Wednesday, 13 November 1963.

In recent times a wide array of paranormal activity has been witnessed first hand by both the cinema's staff and paying customers, therefore it is no surprise that a number of paranormal investigations have taken place at this location.

The Derry's Cross area, where Reel Cinema is situated today, is known to be paranormally active; there is documentation stating that at least three burial grounds were once located within this small area. One of these old burial grounds was used as a final resting place for Napoleonic prisoners of war. It is also quite common for building ground works in this area to be stopped and delayed due to human remains having been unearthed.

Previous paranormal activity

Screen Two in the cinema seems to be one of the most active areas, as the full manifestation of a woman in white has been seen at the back of the screen room.

Another female shade sits in a particular seat on one of the front rows in Screen Two, although during the screening of films the mysterious woman vanishes into thin air. A number of paying customers who have sat in this seat afterwards comment on having felt watched, of feeling uneasy and sometimes becoming suddenly quite ill and having to leave Screen Two.

The ladies' toilets are reported to be very active, from feelings of being watched to loud unexplainable noises – to name but a few.

I have personally had the pleasure of taking part in two separate all-night paranormal investigations at the Reel Cinema.

My first night vigil at the Reel Cinema, then known as the ABC, took place on Friday, 28 April 2006. I led a team of sixteen paranormal investigators to uncover the truth behind the hauntings at this impressive building.

George Street. with Plymouth Theatre Royal on the right. (Courtesy of Derek Tait)

On Friday, 16 October 2009, I returned to undertake an all-night paranormal investigation at the Reel Cinema with Supernatural Investigations (UK) team. The following is an actual report of events which was written by my friend and fellow Supernatural Investigations (UK) investigator, Francesca Haydon.

I was excited about this investigation. I knew nothing at all about the building and had never even heard of it as I don't live in the area. Before the investigation, I pondered on how it might feel to go to a building which had shown so many films, cinema being a great interest of mine and of course being designed to evoke emotions. I wondered about stone tape theory and the idea that many powerful emotions would have been experienced over the years by individuals who might have been scared by horror films, weeping at love stories, and generally moved by powerful images and stories, and I wondered whether some of this emotion might have been captured within the fabric of the building. My first impression of the building was that it reminded me of my childhood. It looked like cinemas I remember going to at that time and brought back feelings of excitement and pleasure. It was lovely to see that the building had been kept as it had been and not too heavily modernised. Arriving at the cinema was a little like going back in time and this captured my imagination.

The Reel Cinema at night.

Screen One was our base area and, prior to setting up equipment, I sat in the auditorium, noticing any impressions. I had the impression of the area being used during the Second World War as some kind of gathering area, perhaps during air raids, and as temporary accommodation for those whose houses had been bombed and to organise refugees waiting to be homed. I also had the image of wounded people, as I could see bloodied bandages and people being nursed. Another image I had was of a large volume of water filling the building. I did wonder whether I might be tuning in to a showing of *Titanic*, but on reflection this might have been dowsing with water following a fire. I would not categorically assert that these were psychic impressions but may simply have been my imagination. Nevertheless, I would be interested to know if they match the history.

I noticed as I sat in Screen One that the acoustics of the building seemed a little unusual. Sound carries and seems to come from a different area from that which it originates. It was also possible in some parts of the building to hear noises from outside. At one point I even heard a scream, which I believe came from outside. We were joined for the night by three cinema staff members and three guests, all of whom were made very welcome and I believe enhanced the investigation greatly. The team seemed cohesive, but there were groups of people who knew one another better than others. This can be relevant in terms of the feelings it can evoke and the individual's consequent interpretation of events. Psychologically speaking, people can interpret events and environments metaphorically and in a way which matches their internal state so, for example, if one is feeling angry, one may imagine scenes of anger and confuse this with psychic impressions. This phenomenon is known as projection and is a defence mechanism. There are even theories that strong feelings can cause poltergeist-like activity or catalytic exteriorisation phenomena. I make these general psychological observations in the spirit of an interest in human nature and our relationships with one another and as an alternative, sceptical interpretation of our findings. It is important to the integrity and sophistication of our research to take into account psychological responses to the environment we are working in and the individuals we work alongside.

Séance

We began the investigation with a séance in the foyer, outside the doors to Screens One and Two. The entire group took part in this short séance, designed to open the investigation and invite the spirit presences to come forward and communicate with us. The area was very dark but one could make out the outlines of the other members of the group. During the séance, Jason, who was to my right, appeared in my peripheral vision to transfigure into a lady wearing a bonnet who was looking over her left shoulder and seemed anxious. I kept turning to look at Jason and as my eyes adjusted he became Jason again, but again in my peripheral vision the woman reappeared. I wondered whether she might be an usherette and could not remember whether usherettes wore bonnets. This vision is likely, I believe, to have been explained by my brain making a coherent picture out of something my eyes could not properly see since we can only properly focus on around 15 per cent of an area we are directly looking at. I asked Jason how he felt at the end of the séance and he had not experienced anything so I discounted this experience.

Session One – Ladies' Restroom

This session began at 00:14. Temperature readings were an average of 18°C. We were joined by Duncan (staff member) and Christine (guest) for this session.

Jason said he thought that the cubicle and the main doors would have been heard slamming in this area. He felt that the last cubicle on the left as you face the toilets had an oppressive feeling and that trauma of some sort had taken place there. He also felt that this area was not part of the original building.

At 00:21 Kevin began calling out. He asked for the spirits to generate smells or to touch one of us and to affect Jason and Christine as the sensitives in the team. Christine said that she felt the energy was moving around the room. Jason felt that the cubicle on the far right was currently active and high in energy. Christine said she could hear a lady sobbing and moving briefly through the area as if replaying something. She felt the replay moved from the area in front of the large mirrors towards the cubicles. In response to this Jason said that he had got the name Jayne Vickery during the séance and kept thinking of her. Christine felt that the energy was different by the door coming into the room from the energy she felt just past the pillar.

Jason had the psychic impression of a struggle between a man and woman into the cubicle on the far right. He felt that a man had attacked a woman there in the early 1900s. Jason pictured the man grabbing the woman by the neck and saying, 'You bitch. You bitch,' but he felt that the cubicle was not a cubicle at the time this happened. At this point I asked Jason whether he had a name for this presence and Christine whispered the name Elizabeth to me. Jason said Bob or Bill (a short name). He felt that what he was experiencing was a playback rather than an active presence.

Christine had the sense of someone being pulled by their hair.

Jason had the feeling that he was off balance, as though he were on a ship in front of the cubicles. In the cubicle on the far left Jason saw a stabbing and the image of a knife and blood and of someone having their head bashed in.

Christine had the impression that where we were was once a changing room and Jason thought this had once been a theatre, as he had seen people dancing and walking hand-in-hand. Jason's overall impression was that the toilets were oppressive, but that there were no active presences here at this time.

Duncan (the staff member) said this was the first time he had been into the ladies' toilets and that he had picked up something about someone being grabbed by their right wrist.

Christine said that her throat had felt sore in this area and Jason thought that this tied in with his impression of strangulation or hanging.

Kevin tried calling out and recorded this to try to capture EVP. While he was doing this I had the name Helen come into my head and the surname Earth, which I realised was a lot like 'hell on earth'.

Jason said that a presence called Mary might be seen standing in the doorway to the right cubicle as they first enter the room. He described her as being blonde and wearing a white dress or ballgown.

The session ended at 00:43.

It was interesting that the restrooms evoked so many scenes of violence. One explanation for this is that through group contagion the group imagined more and more scenes of violence as they influenced one another's imaginations. One might also expect that toilets are a likely place for these events to occur because they are more private than the larger areas of the building. I did notice that the cubicles felt different to the rest of the room. There were square bars on the windows, which looked a little eerie in the dark. One is detached from the group slightly when in a cubicle and this raises anxiety.

Session Two – Screen One

This session began at 00:49. We began at the top of the auditorium and worked our way down. We all noted that orbs were being captured on our digital cameras.

Jason had a feeling that one of the chairs in the centre at the top pops up and down on its own. Jason had the impression of a projectionist, a man who is tall, thin and gaunt and called Tom. He felt Tom would have been felt by the door at the back of the room and that people would have looked behind them because they would have had the feeling that someone was there. He felt the presence was from the 1920s or '30s, but his clothes looked more like 1940s or '50s. I suggested that he may have worked there for a period spanning all this time.

I noted how dark it was at the top of Screen One and that it was only possible to see people when they were very close. I think this could raise anxiety and cause a feeling of being crept up on.

We heard a noise like a tap dripping to the left at the bottom of the room. Duncan said he thought this was likely to be the speakers cooling down. I also heard a scream, which I believe came from the street outside.

At the front or bottom of this room Jason said that he felt happy in this area and could see people enjoying plays. Jason had the feeling of wanting to lie down in the middle at the front and he did so. He explained that this feeling is usually associated with someone being killed or falling over. Jason had the impression of a seven or eight-year-old boy, who he also thought was named Tom. He felt he would be running around and that he is an active presence. He described the boy as having a short, brown bowl-haircut and that he was from the early 1900s. He was playful and intrigued by us. Jason thought he might be responsible for chairs moving up and down on their own. He also thought he may have been heard laughing.

Jason tried calling out and then Jason, Kevin, Duncan and I did a tech neutral séance around the EMF (Electromagnetic Field) meter, which was on the floor between us. I had the impression of an aggressive man standing very close to me on my left-hand side during the séance. I noticed that my shadow was being cast upon the curtains beside me and that this may have triggered my imagination and caused the thought that a man was standing beside me. We heard a door slam during the séance and Duncan felt this could have been caused by a backdraft. Jason said that he had a name like Carolyn, Caroline or Carol-Ann during the séance.

The temperature in this area dropped a little during the session from 20°C to 19.3°C but this was not felt to be significant.

Break

During the break which followed this session I was speaking to Jason in front of the hub, which was at the top of the stairs as you enter Screen One. I turned to look at Jason and thought I saw the door at the top of the auditorium close, out of the corner of my eye. I think this was caused by my being tired and also by the light reflecting on the blue glossy paint on the door, which gave the effect of movement as I turned my head. It may also have been caused by autosuggestion, because Jason had mentioned the impression of the projectionist being sensed in that area. Jason also told me that during the break they had tried to make some dust appear in the ladies' restrooms to debunk the orbs being captured on the infrared camera there. They had done this by jumping up and down. After this Jason reported that the EMF was registering high readings and I suggested that jumping on the carpet may have caused static electricity.

Session Three – Screen Two

This session began at 01:41. We checked the trigger object, which was placed in the hope of getting some kind of interaction from whatever may be haunting the location, but it had not moved..

Jason paced back and forth for some time in the area just in front of the screen. He felt that this was linked with an active male presence who does this and who also may give people the feeling that they are being rushed at or rushed past when going up and down the stairs. Jason felt the male was the host of a show and that he was pacing with anxiety because he was worried that something may go wrong. Jason did disclose that he had just had a cup of coffee, but he did not think this had caused the need to pace. Jason felt the presence was from the mid-1800s and that he was called Richard. Jason also had the impression that there was a stage here. Jason felt the presence died of a heart attack because he was overdoing it. I noted to myself that Christine had told us she was a cardiac nurse and wondered whether this might be either affecting Jason in terms of autosuggestion or whether the presence was drawn to Christine. In this area I again had the impression of a large volume of water entering the building and I wondered whether there had been a fire here. The name Jack came into my head at this point.

At 01:50 Kevin called out. He thought he saw a flicker of light to his right while sitting in the middle at the top of the auditorium.

Jason said that he thought that Screens One and Two had once been one room, as he wanted to pace through the wall.

Jason picked up on an elderly lady called Annie, who died here.

We conducted a séance at the front by the screen, again using only the EMF, which was placed on the floor between us. Christine described the presence of a lady in a long white dress with red hair. She described the lady as being in a spotlight, mesmerised and unable to sing because of stage fright. She described her as having 'weird, Betty Davis eyes' and being pretty but like a rabbit caught in headlights. Christine felt the presence of a lady behind her during the séance who was afraid to come forward. During the séance people felt hot and cold draughts. Kevin said he had picked up on the name Mary.

Session Four – Screen Three

This session began at 02:21. I sat near the back of the auditorium. This was a much smaller room than the other two screens. I was beginning to feel tired at this point and noticed that the energy in the group seemed to drop a little, which is normal for that time of night.

Jason said that during the tour he had picked up an old gentleman in this area near the back of the room on the left. He felt his name was George and that he had died peacefully here during a film in the 1970s or '80s. Jason said he felt calm and thought nothing much had happened here. I also noticed that the screen had newer chairs in it than the rest of the cinema, which might have given the impression that the room was not as old as the rest of the building and therefore did not have such an interesting history.

Kevin was sitting at the front of the room and reported feeling depressed.

Christine, who was sitting at the back on the left-hand side, said that she could smell tobacco. Jason said that he thought George smoked a pipe. Jason said George was wearing a brown tweed jacket and Christine and Kevin exclaimed that they had had the same image. Jason felt that George really enjoyed films, especially comedies, and that he might be heard laughing. Christine felt that George came here alone because his wife had died and because he used to come here with her. She got the place name Yelverton in connection with George. Jason felt he was a nice man who had become isolated later in life. Christine described him as stocky and barrel-chested. Kevin suggested putting the EMF where the group thought George was, at the back of the auditorium on the left in row H. Jason went to do this and saw that the first seat was partially down, barring his entrance to the row. Christine, who was sitting in row H, said the seat was not down when she had entered the row because she would have had to go around it. She felt George had put the seat down to prevent Jason entering the row because he was enjoying her company. Christine felt George had had a farm in Yelverton called Bullers Farm and that at first George had shown her some bulls. Jason felt that George might press the backs of people's chairs if they were noisy, to shut them up. Christine also felt that horses were linked with George.

Séance

The group took part in a séance in the ladies' restrooms, which was felt to be the most interesting area. The séance began at 03:08. I stood out but the rest of the group took part. I chose to do this in order to be free to debunk. An EMF meter was placed on a table in the middle of the group. The temperature for the room was between 19.8°C and 20.8°C at the start of the session. Little was happening so I suggested that the group shuffle over to the area nearer the toilets, as this was felt during our session to be more significant than the other part of the room. As the group moved they also took the table with them by nudging it with their feet. The EMF meter began to sporadically light up over the next few minutes and we could find no clear explanation for this, although Duncan did say he thought that cables may be beneath the area. There was also a voice recorder beside it. We had a lot of interference on radios throughout the night, which would suggest that a lot of radio interference was present (e.g. from people driving taxis) and I wondered whether this might have an impact. On discussion with Damian, we also noted that there can be natural fluctuations in EMF levels. I did not feel that the lights were occurring in response to any given questions by the group. The group moved the table back to its original position and the lights died down. We also removed and turned off all mobile phones and radios from people's pockets. If there are high levels of EMF at times in the area this might explain people reporting activity, because they may in fact be experiencing auditory and visual hallucinations with natural causes.

Kevin reported that in the doorway to the room he felt colder than when he was nearer the centre of the room. He may have been in a draught but in fact the temperature in the room by the end of the session had risen to an average of 24°C (24.6°C beside Kevin). This steep rise in temperature can probably be attributed to a large number of people being in a small area. The other team said they had picked up on a presence called Mary in the toilets and the group called out to her. I noted that our group (Kevin) had also picked up a Mary but did not say so until we held our debrief. This session ended at 03:35.

Following this session I spent some time in the foyer area from 03:38 with Jason, Richard and Clare. While looking through the open door into Screen One I saw a flash of white light. We moved into Screen One from 03:49. Jason said that the names Marilyn and May were relevant to this area (May being attached to Screen Three). Jason also felt that someone had been following him all night.

I sat halfway up the auditorium in the middle and Damian stood still in front of the screen. In the low light Damian appeared to be moving when he was not. This was an interesting effect which I believe may debunk some experiences had in this area; because the light was low and the distance between us was quite large, I believe that Damian appeared to move because I was unable to focus on him properly. It is known that the eyes are unable to stay still on something even when we stare at it and this is one explanation for the appearance of auras.

This marked the end of a fantastic night in a location steeped in history. I do hope we will have the opportunity to visit Reel Cinema again. I would like to express my gratitude to Duncan at Reel Cinema and his team for allowing us access to the location and thanks to Kevin for organising a very enjoyable investigation.

Poppy's Guesthouse

In 2009, the Supernatural Investigations (UK) team took part in an all-night vigil at Poppy's Guesthouse, located upon Plymouth's historic Hoe, on All Hallow's Eve, when it is believed that the veil between this world and the next is at its thinnest.

The investigation team arrived just after 9 p.m. and we set up the technical equipment to prepare for our all-night vigil.

The team had a very productive night, with the group's psychic picking up on some prominent information that was confirmed as being relevant to the past and current paranormal activity that has been experienced first hand by the owner and her guests, including phantom smells that manifested from nowhere, a member of the team feeling touched on the arm, and another having their clothing pulled quite erratically by an invisible force. Cold spots were also recorded, along with a great deal of EVP (Electronic Voice Phenomenon) and video footage. Of course, as always, the team investigated thoroughly all other possibilities for these so-called paranormal occurrences, but the team could not rule out that they may have indeed encountered a wide array of paranormal activity during their time spent at this location.

My friend and Supernatural Investigations (UK) Core Team Investigator, Francesca Haydon, wrote the following report, which includes actual events that occurred during the Supernatural Investigations (UK) investigation at Poppy's Guest House on Halloween 2009.

Adopting, amongst other perspectives, a sceptical line of enquiry to our findings enhances the standard of our research. In taking into account both a believer's perspective which seeks to evidence the continuous existence of the human soul, and a number of other perhaps more sceptical explanations, we offer participants and reviewers the opportunity to reach their own conclusions while in possession of a wide scope of possibilities. One sceptical position one can take is to consider psychological responses to the environment we are working in and the individuals we work alongside, and the impact these might have upon what we experience and how we interpret these experiences. In attempting this task it is not, of course, possible for me to adopt a detached psychological analysis because I am myself a participant. I adopt an ethnographic participant observer position and offer all my observations in the spirit of passion for human nature and our relationships with one another. These tentative parapsychological explanations I offer are, I believe, evidence of fascinating phenomena of an alternative kind.

We set up our base in the dining room and this was also where we held our opening séance and first session. The group was small, with only five of us plus our hostess, Diane,

so we did not split into teams for most of the night but instead formed one group. The roles were adjusted at the beginning of the night. The group seemed happy and relaxed and chatted on arrival and shared a pot of tea kindly provided by Diane, the guesthouse owner. Diane was careful not to give too much information about the history of the building or the experiences reported. None of the group had been to the guesthouse before.

Poppy's Guesthouse.

Dining Room

After an initial tour we began our séance in the dining room, which had been negotiated as an interesting place to hold the séance. The group joined hands and I personally felt quite calm. Diane had told us during the tour that she was already feeling affected. During the tour, Diane explained when the building had been constructed and roughly how and when it had been modified.

Kevin said at the start of this session that he had the impression of a coffin in the room, as though someone had been laid out here. This is the kind of statement which can raise anxiety but I did not personally see any evidence of this. During the séance I kept my eyes open and I saw Diane fall forwards twice. The second time I let out a shriek because I thought she was going to fall. Diane seemed unaffected by this and said that she had felt as though she were being pushed forward by a spirit who was shouting 'I'm Annie' at her. I suggested she keep her eyes open for safety reasons to aid her balance. Following the séance, Kevin dowsed and picked up on a spirit called Annie, although he himself admitted that this may have been caused by autosuggestion. If you believe, as I do, that it is the dowser's unconscious driving micro-movements which move dowsing rods then, alongside autosuggestion, Kevin may also have had a desire (not necessarily conscious) to agree with our hostess so as to maintain group cohesion. Diane asked whether she had known Annie in a past life in the house, and disclosed that she believed she had lived here in a past life and had been drawn to live here in this life.

Attic Rooms

During this session Kevin asked me to do some dowsing, which I did, and we kept apart, dowsing in separate rooms. I have not done any dowsing for a while, although I have completed a training course in it and have experience doing it during investigations. Nevertheless, I was nervous about doing this and about the idea that the group would compare our results. Although I find I can get results from dowsing, I am unsure about the validity of the information I am gathering. I think there is a strong possibility that the information is imagined and I am not sure how I would know if it were not. Nevertheless, I like to remain open-minded. My belief is that the information gathered through dowsing, at least in my case, is delivered via tiny micro-movements from my unconscious. In other words, I am not consciously moving the dowsing rods in any particular way and usually cannot predict their answers to my questions, but I believe that my unconscious is determining the answers. My unconscious may be receiving the information from spirit, autosuggestion, my imagination, or residual imprints left upon an environment which leads to guesses. I do not pretend to know which of these, or indeed which combination of these factors, could be at play, and there may be further possible explanations also.

It seems that I was gathering information about a family named Edwards whom Kevin named in the first session ('Annie' was an 'Edwards' according to his results in session 1). The dates I have given appear to add up with the relationships between the different family members. I would imagine there is some possibility that the family could be traced through research if they do indeed exist.

We de-briefed this session immediately afterwards and I was interested to find that there was very little correlation between my results and Kevin's. We were clearly exploring different time periods, which might explain the lack of correlation, but as each of us dowsed for spirit presences and gave a count of how many presences were in the area at the present time, unless the spirits left and new ones arrived between us switching rooms, then at least one of us has to be wrong in my view. I am fully willing to assume this is me, as Kevin has a much better track record than I do! However, this lack of correlation does lead me to doubt the validity of dowsing per se. The group were keen to focus on one correlation – that both Kevin and I had picked up on twins, which is not a common finding. I was not able to spot any cue in the environment which might have led to us both finding twins through autosuggestion. The team were keen to validate the finding by saying that twins run in families and wondering whether the two sets of twins might have been related. Later on I dowsed again in Room 6 and confirmed that the twins were related. When I asked Kevin to do the same, we again disagreed. The focus on the hit of 'twins' in my view represented a confirmation bias or a desire in the group to confirm the belief that we were indeed in the presence of spirits with whom we had communicated. But when comparing our results, which contain more misses than hits, there is really more evidence to dispute this notion.

Downstairs Bedroom

During this session the group seemed buoyant and relaxed. Kevin picked up on a likeable man named Charles and became quite giggly around this pleasant character. The group were clearly fantasising when they were imagining the sunlight flowing into the room during the daytime. There was a hit when Kevin said that the area in the centre of the room seemed busy and Diane said that people have seen spirits walking through the centre of the room. When Kevin spoke of a table in the middle of the room I imagined séances taking place in the room, which is reasonably likely as this was a popular Victorian parlour game.

Lounge/Kitchen

We were aware that Diane's son was asleep in the lounge so we concentrated on the kitchen. My feeling was that the group were tiring at the time as this session lacked energy. There was a good hit when Kevin said that in the office/parlour area he could sense an Anderson shelter. Diane said that a few feet away, next door had excavated an air-raid shelter in the same area of their garden. This led to powerful imagined images for me of people in great fear sheltering from German air raids.

Diane's Bedroom

The group noted that there were very high EMF readings at the foot of Diane's bed and these seemed to be emanating from the floor, where, directly beneath, we believe the strip light in the kitchen to be. We explained to Diane that high EMF readings are allegedly associated with visual and auditory hallucination.

Kevin correctly targeted an area of the room as being significant and Diane told us that on that side of the bed both she and her son, about two years apart, had been poked in the middle of the night whilst sleeping. It is possible that through unconscious communication Diane had suggested an aversion to that side of the room. I noted that when she sat on her bed she sat on the opposite side and she told us that she now sleeps on that side of the bed because of what happened. Psychological explanations are often offered to those who experience disturbance during the night, including, of course, unrecalled nightmares and hypnagogic hallucination, and I offer these tentatively and only for consideration. Hallucinations can be very vivid and somatisation is similarly felt powerfully, and both appear to have an exterior cause. One interesting claim which strongly disputes these theories as an explanation for what Diane reported is that both her and her son had the same experience on the same side of the bed. Diane did admit that her son might have heard her talking about her experience, which could have caused autosuggestion, but the time lapse between their two experiences makes autosuggestion perhaps a little less likely. Kevin felt that the spirit of a young man had tried to make himself known to them and I will not actively dispute this claim, I simply offer alternative possibilities.

Room 3

This room was the most interesting for me and this may simply be because Kevin noted on the tour that he had strong feelings in here. Kevin informed us through his dowsing that an unhappy elderly female inhabited the room, especially in the corner, which is screened off. Being unable to access or see an area can lead to a little anxiety, and this might be why we were focussed on this area. Several times in this room I caught a waft of urine. This was shortly afterwards smelt by Emma and Kevin, although this may of course have been contagion. I was sitting close to an open window and Emma and Kevin were slightly further away. I asked Diane whether the smell might be coming from outside, but she could think of no reason why this might be. Diane had mentioned that the smell of lily of the valley had been noticed in the house, and this smelt acidic, just like urine. My experience was fuelled by Kevin's dowsing results and I began to develop an impression of a neglected elderly lady in poor health who was not being cared for, to which I attached the smell of urine. As the group built up the image, group contagion was fairly obvious. Kevin said the presence was angry. Diane then told us that the mirror on the wall outside the room had fallen off the wall, but the hook it was on had remained intact. The group added these perhaps unrelated incidents together to form a chain of events which confirmed the belief that a spirit is present. Emma stated that the woman was an outcast who hated the sight of herself and this again added fuel to the image we were generating. I also remembered that Diane had said she cleared the room because she felt abuse had taken place in here. It is impossible to tell whether we were genuinely picking up on a presence or residual energy, or whether the group, through contagion, were generating the image together through imagination.

During the vigil Kevin felt his shirt being tugged, and during the séance we held in this room I felt both my arms touched, one after another. I was standing in the same area Kevin had stood in when his shirt had been pulled. It felt as though a drop of water had landed on each arm. No one from the group could have touched me because we were all holding hands and I could not see anything which could have landed on me. Sometimes in a situation like that, where visual distraction is limited by the lights being off, we can increase our awareness of natural bodily sensations and read meaning into them because of the situation (i.e. we are doing a séance and asking spirits to affect us). This is certainly a possibility. The sensation, of course, felt absolutely real, but it was a subjective experience and can be interpreted in various ways. I was also tired and had my arms out to hold hands with Emma and Clare, which might perhaps have caused twitching as I maintained this position, although this explanation was not consistent with my subjective experience.

Following this session, during free time, I returned to Room 7 in the attic with Damian and again smelt urine shortly after entering. I began to worry that the smell was emanating from me and asked Damian to check, but he assured me I did not smell! The spiritual explanation might be that the spirit of the lady followed me upstairs.

I am very grateful to both Diane and Kevin for this fantastic opportunity to investigate a very interesting building. We had some fascinating results and experiences with multiple possible explanations.

Palace Theatre, 121-123 Union Street

This building was known as the New Palace Theatre of Varieties and, more recently, The Academy nightclub. Built in 1898 for the Livermore Brothers, this impressive building is one of only a handful of Victorian buildings left in Plymouth today. It was designed by architects Wimpers and Arber as a music hall and variety theatre.

The theatre opened as the New Palace Theatre on Union Street on Monday, 5 September 1898. In its heyday the building would have hosted around 2,500 people. The auditorium consisted of stalls and a pit, with a grand circle and gallery to suite, along with a further eight stage boxes.

Sadly, the original lavish auditorium and stage house were completely destroyed in a serious fire on 23 December 1898, almost four months after the theatre opened. Out of the ashes the theatre was restored and re-opened to the public.

This well-known Plymouth landmark has had numerous owners during its long service, and was once owned by the Hoyles family. Legend has it that the spirit of Mrs Hoyle haunts the Palace Theatre.

It is said that a woman called Mary, who supposedly passed away in the fire of 1898, haunts the vacant ruins of the Palace Theatre today. I have spoken to a couple of individuals in recent times about the famous theatre. One particular gentleman, who worked as a security guard here in the late 1980s, told me that he had a number of unnerving encounters during his employment at the ancient theatre. The gentleman recalled one particular morning, around 3 a.m., when the building was closed for business. He and a colleague were talking when all of a sudden the peace was shattered by the sound of a disembodied female scream, followed by all the lights going off – leaving both men open-mouthed in the dark. The gentleman went on to state that noises were quite commonplace and the sighting of dark silhouettes resembling human forms were also seen by himself and others in areas unoccupied at the time.

The New Palace Theatre, Union Street.

The impressive Victorian mural on the wall at the New Palace Theatre.

The New Palace Theatre, Union Street, built in 1898. (Courtesy of John Van der Kiste)

Today the Palace Theatre is no longer open, although I would jump at the opportunity to spend the entire night at this awe-inspiring building, just to find out if any old souls still tread the boards here.

Peverell's Haunted House

My friend and fellow Supernatural Investigations (UK) paranormal investigator, Clare Buckland, experienced a wide array of spooky experiences whilst living in an old Victorian house in Peverell. Clare has kindly provided an account of the paranormal happenings that occurred at this location:

> I first came to live in the South West in 1995. I had accepted a place at the University of Plymouth studying Ecology and Ocean Science. During my first year in Plymouth I had to live in a very large tower block hall situated on campus. While this was a great way to meet people and stumble out of bed and make it to my lectures within ten minutes, it was unfortunately an awful building, resembling all the warmth and charisma of a hospital ward.

Towards the end of my first year, a group of friends and I decided that we should rent a student house. We were being evicted from halls to make way for the forthcoming freshers [first year students]. We found a large six-bedroom Victorian house in an area of Plymouth near Mutley. It was beautiful, had loads of room, three bathrooms, high ceilings, wooden floors, a garden and it was affordable. We managed to scrape together the huge deposit and first month's rent in advance and come September we had a new home.

Jude was going on holiday the week before lectures, so she moved in first and set up her room, only to return home to Bristol the next day. Next, Sue and John moved in (they wanted a head start on finding those elusive student jobs in town). I returned from Bury a few days later with my Mum and Dad and a carload of gear. They were impressed. Mum was happy it was warm, dry and nicely decorated and Dad was just glad to be out of the car after our five-hour journey.

Mum had an accident ten years ago which damaged her lower spine and, as a consequence, she now has to walk with crutches. My bedroom was on the second floor, so Jude (who had one of the ground floor rooms), suggested they sleep in her room. Everything was decided and we all set off for bed. About fifteen minutes later I heard the unmistakable sound of my Mum coming up the stairs. My Dad was following behind with a duvet and pillows.

'What's wrong?' I asked.

'Your father won't sleep in that room,' replied Mum.

'Why?'

Early photograph of Mutley Plain. (Courtesy of Derek Tait)

Two early views of Mutley Plain, Plymouth.

'Because he said it's cold and he doesn't like the feeling in there,' said Mum. It had been a very long day and, not wanting to argue, they had my bed and I slept on an airbed on the floor.

The next morning, Dad explained that while Mum had gone off to use the bathroom he had got into bed. He lay there relaxing for a while with his eyes shut. He then got the impression that someone was standing over the bed staring at him. It freaked him out and that's why they came upstairs. Now, my Dad is no fool and he adores my Mum, so he wouldn't have asked her to struggle up four flights of stairs for no good reason. Mum said that she knew something had frightened Dad and that it was a good reason to sleep elsewhere. I should point out that my Mum and Dad have had some very spooky experiences over the years and Mum is quite psychic.

This was the first of many strange experiences in the house, which included:

† Bumps and bangs – one very loud crash came from John's bedroom one evening and it sounded like his wardrobe had fallen over. On investigation, we found that nothing was out of place or had toppled over

† Feeling like you were being watched – especially in the kitchen

† Kitchen cupboard doors would always be found open, even after closing them properly. You could leave the room and return in under a minute and they would have opened again without a sound

† Mysterious footsteps on the stairs and landings. I would often think a friend was coming upstairs only to find no one there

† Jude's room (the one my Dad didn't like) was perpetually cold, even with the heating on full and no obvious draughts

† Twice, while in my room studying, I heard voices downstairs. I would go down expecting to see some of my housemates but there was no one there

† Amy twice saw shadowy outlines at upstairs windows when she knew everyone was out of the house

When our twelve-month lease was up, we decided to move (not surprising) into a different house. The people who moved into our old house were friends of friends and I often bumped into them in our local pub. Having heard nothing of our experiences, one night they told Sue and I about the things they had experienced in that house. It was almost funny to hear three twenty-something, pool-playing, beer-drinking lads recount these strange tales with such honesty and emotion. One of them said he was thinking of moving in with his girlfriend and another said he never stayed in the house alone.

Years passed peacefully and we all graduated with honours. I am still in contact with many old university chums, but Sue is my best friend. She is now a police officer with the Devon and Cornwall Constabulary, is married and has a little boy (my godson). They still live in Plymouth and although our lives are very different now, we still reminisce about our university days. We have never forgotten our year in that house and Sue told me that it has since been converted into three flats.

Six months ago and almost ten years since we lived in the house, Sue told me a story, one I had never heard before and one that took two bottles of wine for her to pluck up the courage to tell. During the Christmas holidays of that fateful year, Sue had been working at WH Smith in town. She wanted a part-time job and thought that showing loyalty over the Christmas period would win them round. Her parents only lived in Dorset so she could travel home after work on Christmas Eve and come back on the 27th of December. This meant that she had to stay in the house on her own, as we had

Above & below: *Mutley Plain today.*

all returned to our parents for the holidays. She hated staying there alone, though never told us about what happened during that week. She had got into the habit of turning on all the downstairs lights, switching on the TV in the lounge and the radio in the kitchen (even whistling to herself) until there was plenty of background noise.

Lying in bed at night she would often hear footsteps upstairs walking along the landing and into bedrooms. Luckily, she had no need to go upstairs at all because her bedroom was on the ground floor and there was a bathroom at the back of the kitchen. One night she woke up with an urgent need to use the bathroom. She got up, put on the bedroom light, opened the door and put on the hall light. As she made her way to the kitchen door she walked past the bottom of the stairs and, out of the corner of her eye, she saw a pair of legs about four or five steps up. They were wearing trousers and boots. She stopped, closed her eyes and turned. When she opened her eyes seconds later the legs had gone, but she saw movement further up the stairs, as if someone was walking back up to the landing. This frightened her so much that she packed up her things and went to her Mum's the very next day.

Sue told me that she had kept quiet because she just wanted to forget it happened and knew she would have to return to the house. This explained why she never stayed there on her own again, always went to bed about thirty minutes before everyone else, and was the one who suggested we move at the end of term.

Sue's story reminded me that if you sat in a certain place in the lounge, you could see right across the hall and up the stairs. Whenever anyone sat there they would quickly look up and to their left (in the direction of the stairs). I caught Amy doing this once and when I asked what she saw, she replied, 'I just thought I saw someone standing there on the stairs.' Did Amy and our houseguests see the same thing that scared Sue?

I often wonder if the conversion into flats has changed the experiences of the current occupants, or if they also have some spooky stories to tell?

The Phoenix Public House

I recently had a most intriguing conversation with a gentleman who was landlord of the Phoenix public house in the 1980s.

At about three o'clock one morning he awoke from his well-earned sleep to the deafening sound of the building's alarm system, which had been set off, thus indicating that someone was downstairs in the main bar area. The landlord immediately contacted the police, who arrived within a few minutes. The landlord and the police carried out a thorough search of the building, only to find the pub empty – although during the search it was discovered that the alarm had been tripped by the trapdoor in the floor behind the main bar, which was found fully open and the light leading down into the area below was on. This was most odd as the landlord was absolutely certain that the trapdoor was shut and the light turned off before he ventured up to bed.

The gentleman told me that he once owned a cat whilst living in this property, and for some reason the cat would never venture down the trapdoor, even though as a general consensus cats are very inquisitive animals. He decided one day to go down the trapdoor with his feline friend in his arms, but as soon as the cat realised its fate it jumped from its owner's arms, hissing and spitting profusely. It was quite evident that the cat had no wish to go into this area. One wonders, was there something of a sinister nature lurking below the trapdoor?

Left: *The Phoenix.*

Below: *Union Street, Plymouth.*

As an aside, the landlord recalled a tale from the Second World War, when an American serviceman was involved in a fight in Union Street, just a short distance from the Phoenix. After the fight had dispersed, the seriously beaten serviceman was brought into the bar, where he sadly passed away from the injuries that he had sustained during the fight.

Plymouth Hoe and Sir Francis Drake

The statue of Sir Francis Drake on Plymouth Hoe was unveiled by Lady Elliot Drake on 14 February 1884. It commemorates Plymouth's Elizabethan hero, who was born at Crowndale Farm, south of Tavistock, in 1540.

Sir Francis Drake is associated with many ghost stories and folktales in both Plymouth and the county of Devon. Therefore I would like to tell you of some of the hauntings and legends connected with the great Elizabethan Admiral.

Sir Francis Drake once gave Plymouth a fresh water supply; apparently he whispered some magical words over a spring on ancient Dartmoor. The spring is said to have turned into a raging river of fresh water, which followed him back to the town of Plymouth.

Drake is supposed to have sold his soul to Satan at Devil's Point, a rough outcrop of headland that can be found overlooking the mouth of Devonport. It was from this very point in 1588 that Drake and his witches supposedly conjured up a devastating storm that drove the Spanish Armada North and West to their doom. It is believed that if you were to visit Devil's Point in the early hours of a July morning, when the fog is rolling in off Plymouth Sound, you may hear disembodied voices chanting. These are supposedly the restless sprits of Drake and his witches uttering their incantations and spells.

Another magical tale tells of how Drake whittled on a wooden stick at Devil's Point. Every shaving of wood that landed upon the water was immediately transformed into a fire ship that was known to have caused chaos and a fiery death to the Spanish Armada.

Plymouth Hoe, a favourite haunt for Sir Francis Drake.

The ghost of the local hero can be found haunting The Ship Inn in Exeter. This old tavern was a favourite haunt for Drake and a number of his seafaring colleagues, although Drake was actually barred due to his drunken behaviour. This, however, has not stopped the illustrious Drake returning to haunt the Ship Inn. I have had the pleasure of spending the entire night investigating this location, but can confirm that we were unsuccessful that night in having a close encounter with Drake's nebulous spirit.

Drake's Drum resides at Buckland Abbey, a former home of the great Admiral. This drum accompanied Drake when he circumnavigated the globe between 1577 and 1580. Legend has it that should England ever be in danger from a foe, Drake's drum will beat and he will return again to defend her shores. Apparently, the drum was heard beating out a ghostly tattoo when the German fleet surrendered in 1918.

View from the Hoe across Plymouth Sound and Drake's Island.

Boringdon Hall is another favourite haunt for Sir Francis Drake, who has been sighted in the Great Hall wearing his armour, complete with sword.

A phantom figure resembling Drake has been witnessed upon Plymouth Hoe, gazing out to sea. It is of no surprise that Drake's ghost has been sighted in this area as legend has it that Drake insisted on completing his game of bowls here before he took to sea, even though the top sails of the Spanish Armada were visible off the Devon coast.

Portland Square

Air-raid shelter complex number 34 was built by Plymouth City Council in preparation for the outbreak of the Second World War. The shelter was to be constructed near to Drake's reservoir. The trenches for the air-raid shelter were excavated and work took place between August and November 1939. The completed design of the subterranean tunnels measured a mere 1.9m high by 1.4m wide, giving you an idea of the standing room in the main tunnel complex.

The Portland Square air-raid shelter was tested to its limit on Saturday, 6 July 1940, when the first bombs were dropped on the city. In just seven nights the following year the centres of Plymouth and Devonport were laid to ruin. The devastating German air raids of the nights of March 20th and 21st and April 21st, 22nd, 23rd, 28th and 29th have become termed the Plymouth Blitz.

Plymouth during the Blitz in the Second World War. (Courtesy of Derek Tait)

Commemorating victims of the air raids during the Second World War. (Courtesy of Derek Tait)

Aftermath of an air raid over the city. (Courtesy of Derek Tait)

The War Memorial on Plymouth Hoe.

On the night of 23/24 April 1941, Plymouth saw the worst disaster of the Blitz, when the Portland Square air-raid complex took a direct hit during an air raid. It was reported that between seventy-two and seventy-six people lost their lives in this one tragic incident.

Today, a sculpture and plaque reminds us what occurred on that terrible night in 1941, when whole families were wiped out in a single moment.

During one of my regular Haunted Plymouth ghost walks, I had an interesting conversation with a gentleman who informed me that he once lived in the Mary Newman Hall of Residence, an eleven-storey building in the centre of the campus at the University of Plymouth. He went on to say that during his stay at the hall he and a number of his friends had experienced a whole spectrum of strange happenings, including hearing disembodied voices and sounds of an unearthly nature, not to mention the feeling of being watched, even when he was obviously alone on certain occasions.

I have since spoken to a number of people who have stayed at Mary Newman Hall while studying at the university and it seems to be the general consensus that the building is haunted. Individuals have felt inexplicable icy cold blasts of air, as well as an overall feeling of pure dread. The Mary Newman building is situated close to the planetarium and the Portland Square air-raid complex. Could the unusual happenings be linked in any way with the tragic loss of life in 1941? Are the souls from this incident making themselves known to the living, almost seventy years later?

Wyndham Square

Wyndham Square is dominated by St Peter's parish church, an impressive building which also boasts its very own indoor stream. The church was gutted by fire after enemy air raids over Plymouth in 1941, but was rebuilt to its former glory and has recently been subject to a £4 million restoration project. The church tower is a prominent landmark which can be seen towering above the Plymouth skyline. In close proximity to this church is No. 4 Wyndham Square. This building has a more sinister history associated to it.

Local author and friend Derek Tait recalls the chilling tale of the Wyndham Square ghost:

I phoned my partner's dad to see if he could tell me more about the Wyndham Square ghost because he used to live nearby in King Street, Stonehouse at the time. He said that it was a quite well-known story in the 1950s and that people regularly came and went from the house because they heard noises and felt unnerved. One individual reported seeing a strange dog on their bed.

There were also stories of coal mysteriously flying about the premises and the occupiers at the time called upon the assistance of a Church of England priest, as well as a Roman Catholic priest. I've seen this story repeated in the *Herald* at one point; it might have been as long ago as the early 1980s.

When I went to my friend's flat, which was part of No. 4 Wyndham Square, I would hear peculiar noises and the sound of loud banging within the walls, this was back in 1987.

I recall on one particular visit, there was a strange-looking old man who would come out of one of the flats and just stare at me. I asked my friend who he was and he said he didn't know. I didn't find it eerie until some time later, when I started to think more about it and I heard the stories of the hauntings.

three

Outside the City

The Britannia Inn

This inn was the subject of a paranormal investigation after the publican and his family reported seeing silhouettes/shadows moving freely around the vicinity of the bar, before wandering towards the rear hallway that leads to the restrooms. An unseen presence has also been felt in the locality of the pool table.

Also seen on two separate instances by two independent witnesses is the ominous sight of a male figure, standing at least 6ft tall and dressed in clothing dating back to the early 1900s.

The public house had been fitted with a high specification closed circuit television system, which has captured on video what is believed to be one of the suspected spirits. In fact this ghost was captured on not just one CCTV camera, but three separate cameras, if only for a brief second.

The Britannia Inn, Wolseley Road.

Boringdon Hall

'Burth-Y-Don' was the Saxon name given to the impressive Boringdon Hall. The Saxon meaning translates to 'enchanted place on the hill' and this author can confirm that Boringdon Hall is situated in 7 acres of truly stunning Devonshire landscape.

Recorded in the Domesday Book, this striking grade II listed manor house has stood the test of time and is known to have had links with King Henry VIII.

A number of high-profile guests have enjoyed the comforts of Boringdon, including Sir Francis Drake, Sir Walter Raleigh, Richard Grenville and Elizabeth I, who stayed here during her visit to the Westcountry.

Once owned by the Parker family, who were avid supporters of the Crown, they lost Boringdon Hall to Cromwell when it was partly destroyed during the English Civil War.

A fire in March 1989 reduced a large part of the manor house to a smouldering cinder, but once again the ancient manor was raised from the ashes and restored to its former glory.

The following information on Boringdon's haunted history was passed on to me from Debbie Moss, who was at one time the Operations Manager at Boringdon Hall Hotel.

It was around the year AD 956 that King Edgar granted the Manor of Boringdon and Wembury to St Peter of Plympton, so naturally Boringdon Manor belonged to the priory until the Dissolution of the Monasteries in 1539 by Henry VIII.

Boringdon Hall appears to be haunted: if you firmly believe in the paranormal then please read on, and experience our ghost tour.

Left: *Boringdon Hall, a grade II listed manor house. (Courtesy of Stuart Andrews)*

Below: *Coat of Arms at Boringdon Hall. (Courtesy of Stuart Andrews)*

Boringdon Hall at night. (Courtesy of Stuart Andrews)

Upon walking through the grand archway into the hotel, you are greeted by a sixteenth-century suit of armour. With its realistic stance and posture, it won't come as a surprise that many strange happenings are connected with the figure. One particular evening, a night porter was training a newly-appointed replacement porter and they happened to be walking by the figure; as usual the helmet was in the upright position. This was put right, with it in the downward position. Exactly two hours into the evening, which seemed calm for that time of night, the helmet was back to its original position, without anyone being around.

The exact same night the trainee porter, who knew nothing about the hotel's history of spiritual happenings, was walking around the building, in the area looking into the Restaurant Staircase. The shadow he saw moving in a spiral motion towards the top area of the staircase looked almost human-like. As he knew nothing about the reported shadows, he thought it was a customer or the night porter. When getting back together, he explained the situation – both possible explanations were ruled out, as it was early in the morning and the night porter happened to be in the reception area at the time it was seen.

With the land being in ownership for around 900 years, Boringdon Hall Hotel has had a lot of noblemen and women pass through its doors. With it being a newly-reformed hotel, it appears that some of its past visitors are still around and feeling very unsettled.

Room 15

Everyone who knows this building will be familiar with the stories that surround this four-poster bedroom. Many a guest has spent a night in there, and has never felt comfortable with the atmosphere around the window overlooking the Wembury grounds. This could be due to the fact that in the seventeenth century, a young woman fell pregnant with the Lord's son's illegitimate child. The idea of this child being brought up in a respectable family was unheard of at the time. Therefore, to spare the child from torment, the girl fell to her death with the child in her arms. The ghost of a woman and a small child are said to walk outside in the grounds below Room 15.

A popular airline company have stayed within this room, and strange events have occurred. A gentleman has felt something or someone sitting on his chest, making it hard to breath. Alao a pass in a plastic wallet has been placed on the bedside cabinet, and when the owner of the pass awoke, the card was found 10ft across the room, with the plastic wallet in the same position as it was left.

Room 16

Located on the third floor of the main house, Room 16 feels comfortable, but unexplainable happenings within the room do occur. One particular night, a female guest checked into this room. On waking from a deep sleep, she was shocked to discover that her whole body had been turned around, with her feet near the headboard and her head near the foot of the bed. Inexplicably, the woman was still tucked up in bed, eradicating any possibility that she could have been involved.

The Great Hall

In the Great Hall Bar, a tequila bottle once flew off the shelf onto the floor in front of three members of staff.

The Supernatural Investigation (UK) team at Boringdon Hall. (Courtesy of Stuart Andrews)

Activity has been witnessed in various parts of the Great Hall; key sightings of Lady Jane Grey and Sir Francis Drake have been claimed. People sleeping in Rooms 15, 16 and 17 have experienced the feeling of someone sitting on the bed and heard unexplained noises. One visitor is said to have almost fainted in fear of what lay behind the door in Room 15! Another guest sleeping in Room 16 woke to see a dark shadow crossing the room. Strange lights and flashes have been seen by staff and residents. Night porters have also heard loud footsteps and felt cold spots; sometimes the electricity will cut out for no apparent reason, leaving them alone in the dark!

I have had the pleasure of participating in two separate all-night paranormal investigations at this ancient manor house. I include here the following report from my good friend and fellow Supernatural Investigations (UK) investigator Stuart Andrews.

This was a very impressive venue, which also saw a welcome change to recent investigations where we were out in the cold. However, in terms of potential paranormal activity, this was a relatively quiet night for me. That said, it is unrealistic to expect to encounter the unknown each and every time. The following is a summary of what happened in each room, in the order in which our team investigated.

Room 16 – The Mary Rose Room

This was one of the areas from our previous visit, unfortunately this room again proved to be uneventful.

Room 11 – The Elizabeth Room

This was the first of two rooms which seemed to raise my heckles a little during the initial tour of the building.

Perhaps the strangest part was being drawn to what I termed the 'Happy Chair'; for some unusual reason I just felt at peace the three times I sat here and am at a loss to explain this feeling of joy which came from nowhere. In contrast, the area from which this photograph was taken felt exactly the opposite. On switching the lights off, I almost felt unable to continue into the room to this spot, the only time I felt unnerved during the whole investigation. At one point I sat down and, after a little while, returned to the 'Happy Chair' as I felt quite depressed. I understand that Kevin (in the other group) also identified this spot as significant.

The most interesting point was upon leaving, Francesca and I both commented on seeing something move at head height in the same spot, apparently at separate times. We both only volunteered this information at the end of the session and were amazed to find we had both seen something in exactly the same spot, although I was sitting in the chair at the time and Francesca was sitting on the bed. A trick of the light may be ruled out due to our different positions, so it would seem a big coincidence for us both to experience corner-of-the-eye phenomenon in the same spot.

This room also displayed the highest EMF readings of all the bedrooms, although they were explained by lighting and cabling; they were highest at the fireplace and on the pillow area of the bed. Research has now suggested that hand-held EMF meters are

The haunted Elizabeth Room at Boringdon. (Courtesy of Stuart Andrews)

unlikely to accurately identify EIFs (Experience Inducing Fields), which are those of a level shown to commonly induce responses from laboratory participants. However, without very sensitive and complex equipment – which is awkward to work with in the field – a hand-held EMF meter remains a good tool for identifying areas which may offer a possible cause for reported phenomena, particularly in this case, as one of the strongest areas was around both pillows on the room's four-poster bed.

Great Hall

This area looks and feels as if it should be haunted, with the huge crest above the fireplace dominating the room. Again this area was quiet during our time here – surprising really, as one would expect to be a little unnerved given its imposing presence. Indeed, one would expect the two galleries at either end to suggest a feeling of being watched, yet the atmosphere seemed calm and relaxed.

Room 15 – The Isabella Room

Returning to the bedrooms and I'm afraid the pattern of little to report continued; that said, there was an interesting point to note as our guest, Paul, sensed the area outside the door to be significant. On the previous visit one investigator (who was not present on this occasion) reported seeing the door handle move and the door begin to open. He found no one there and by chance I was on my way to this room shortly after the event, so can rule out human interference as I would have passed the culprit on the landing.

The Great Hall at Boringdon. (Courtesy of Stuart Andrews)

We could not recreate the effect, although the investigator concerned reasoned a backdraft as the cause after the night. Sadly this did not make a repeat during this investigation.

Room 14 – The Catherine Room

Members of the group did report experiences in here, although all was quiet for me apart from an unusual feeling of fatigue.

Galleries

The Rose and Grenville Rooms were known to me from a previous visit as being areas that staff disliked or had reported unusual occurrences in, as had some of the groups from the previous investigation in the Minstrel Gallery. So these were areas I was anticipating some action from; however, there was nothing to note.

Room 12 – The Francis Room

This was the other area which caught my attention during the initial walk around; as with Room 11 it was one not covered during our previous night. Perhaps it was too late in the night but nothing really happened in here apart from being mesmerised by the light across the wide, leaded windows while sat on the bed. I did wonder if sightings had been reported here by guests, which might be explained by shadows cast from the trees outside.

Budshead Manor

A few abandoned ruins are all that remain of Budshead manor house, which once stood at the head of Budshead Creek where it joined Tamerton Lake. Although there is very little to see these days, it is said to be the haunt of a menacing spirit known as the White Lady. No one knows her origin, but it is said that she wanders aimlessly around the ruins of the old manor.

Above: *Ruins of the old Budshead manor house.*

Left: *Budshead Creek.*

Clifton Place

In 1964, No. 31 Clifton Place was the scene of pure terror: a family living in the ground floor flat of this 200-year-old house was under siege by a menacing poltergeist.

Pieces of coal were mysteriously appearing and being thrown around the property. The activity increased to the point where the neighbours in the other two flats started to encounter odd happenings too. So much so that all the residents from the house decided to contact their local church, who arranged a visit from one of the church's clergymen. The clergyman did indeed visit the property and witnessed at first hand the coal-throwing poltergeist. The one thing that the clergyman found most baffling was the fact that there was no evidence of coal being present in the property at all, so where was the coal coming from?

Number 31 Clifton Place.

Clifton Place, Plymouth.

The clergyman reported back to his superiors and within a number of weeks an exorcism was conducted to try and rid the property of the restless poltergeist. It did not work, and, as a result, two of the three families living at No. 31 Clifton Place moved out, vowing never to return.

Devonport Dockyard

My good friend and fellow co-founder of Supernatural Investigations (UK), Stuart Andrews, had the honour of spending two consecutive nights investigating the mysterious hauntings associated with the Royal Naval Base at Devonport. Stuart has kindly submitted the following report findings from his time spent at Devonport Dockyard.

On the 28th and 29th of May 2004 the Royal Navy, in conjunction with the Society of Metaphysicians and Brunel University, invited two paranormal groups to spend the weekend in the South Yard Ropery of HM Naval Base Devonport. I was privileged to be invited for this unique event covering two nights, with Becky Andrews joining us for the second night, which allowed an interesting comparison of a fresh pair of eyes, unaware of the first night's findings. The Navy's intention was to use the findings to support the many encounters reported by security, police and base personnel over the years as promotion for their planned visitor centre. The South Yard Ropery was a major production centre for rope and cordage for the entire Royal Navy until its partial destruction by the Luftwaffe in March 1941.

Royal Naval Barracks at Devonport. (Courtesy of Derek Tait)

Devonport is famous for being the largest Naval Base in Western Europe, covering 650 acres, with four miles of coastline within the huge, imposing citadel walls surrounding the base. Within this secure perimeter are fifteen dry docks, five basins and twenty-five tidal berths. Its 2,500 service and civilian personnel and the defence work they undertake is estimated to contribute 10 per cent of the total income for the city of Plymouth. The Devonport flotilla includes fourteen Type 22 and twenty-three frigates, seven Trafalgar class submarines, as well as the Royal Navy's largest ship, HMS *Ocean*, with a displacement of 21,000 tonnes. Devonport is being developed as the Royal Navy's centre for 'Amphibious Excellence', being home to the latest amphibious assault class vessels, HMS *Albion* and HMS *Bulwark*. Both are able to rapidly deliver a substantial payload of Royal Marines, their vehicles and equipment through the next generation of landing craft, to any place in the world as required. The Navy's smallest ship, HMS *Gleaner*, the 25-tonne surveying motor launch, also claims this as its home. The UK Hydrographic Agency, based in Taunton, Somerset and responsible for maritime cartography across the world, also has four of its five survey ships ported here.

Returning to the paranormal investigation, two main areas were the focus of the weekend, with both teams spending a night in each. The first was the Ropemaker's House, a grade II listed building constructed in the late eighteenth century as the home for the Master Ropemaker. Since the Second World War it has been used as a residence for dockyard officials. Over the years it has gained a reputation for being the most haunted house in Plymouth – it certainly looks the part – and on entering you immediately encounter a timeless feeling. Since 2000, however, the building has been vacant and earmarked for development as the proposed visitor centre, a project which, at the time of writing, has suffered further setbacks.

The second area included the surviving Ropery building, a vast multi-storeyed structure built for the production of rope, its huge open areas, similar to those at the Royal Dockyard at Chatham necessary for the production of long lengths of rope and cord. In the dark it was almost impossible to see one end from the other, despite high-powered torches. Near the Ropery and Ropemaker's House is another block of granite-faced buildings, erected in 1766 and originally used as a tarring building. One of the smaller sections is named the Hangman's Cell and was formerly a wheelhouse. According to records, it was the scene of the execution of over 100 (some say as many as 141) French prisoners of war from the Napoleonic era. Somewhat surprisingly, the majority of these executions are believed to have been carried out by the captured French officers, who retained responsibility for maintaining discipline of their men. Life in the services back then was extremely hard, with corporal punishment readily handed out to both Naval and Army personnel on both sides. It is alleged that a nail was driven into the wall for each life taken here, with the hangman from Plymouth attending to oversee the gruesome tasks. Still in situ is what is apparently the only surviving, functioning mechanised trap; above this hangs a noose (presumably of Devonport rope) as a grim reminder of the harsh discipline meted out. The plaque above further detailing:

THIS IS THE EXECUTION CELL USED DURING THE NAPOLEONIC WARS FOR PRISONERS WHO WERE VICTIMS OF THE HARSH LAWS

The Execution Cell. (Courtesy of Stuart Andrews)

Night 1 – Ropemaker's House

After passing security checks, I entered through Cranby Gate and was directed to Flotilla House for a detailed briefing by the Base Commander, Charles Crichton, and a chance to meet the other team. It was then that the realisation of how big and serious a project this was really hit home. Twenty experienced investigators and a comparable number of highly skilled and senior base personnel were all dedicated to spreading out in the search for evidence to support the previously reported spectral encounters. A vast array of equipment was deployed, including the biggest range of trigger objects and experiments I have ever seen at an investigation, justifying the world-wide media coverage that this weekend attracted. Following the base readings and familiarisation of the Ropemaker's House by our team, a rest session was called and a chance to compose our thoughts and adapt our investigation plan to best fit the huge area available. Suddenly ten of us seemed to be way too few! Our team was also lucky enough to be joined by Mr and Mrs T., who had previously resided within the Ropemaker's House. Although details were not disclosed to us until we were halfway through the investigation, their first-hand account of the activity experienced, along with the expertise of the base personnel, really helped us to focus our efforts.

Poltergeist activity has frequently been reported here, with phantom footsteps heard running up the stairs, spectral noises coming from empty third-floor rooms, furniture moving and being overturned. Perhaps most bizarre is the report from previous occupants, who found the work surfaces of the kitchen being torn to shreds overnight. At times the activity has become dangerous, with both children and adults being pushed on the stairs and in the corridors. Sounds from another time have also been reported outside, with the echoes of a horse and carriage being heard bouncing back off the impenetrable granite walls surrounding the base. We certainly gained the impression that these incidents were not isolated to one or two people; many staff have reported encounters from within the house and either refused to enter, or avoided working in particular rooms.

The area where I had the most unusual encounter was on the third (top) floor corridor and the three rooms leading off. Most of us picked up on a heavy, oppressive atmosphere, with a feeling of resistance on certain steps of the staircase leading up to the third floor. A pressing sensation on the chest and shortness of breath were also experienced; this was still present on repeat visits, but not during the vigil held later on in the night or on the Saturday. At 10.50 p.m., once we had returned to Flotilla House, the other team were returning back from the Hangman's Cell with one of them showing clear signs of distress, having apparently been attacked or disturbed in some way by an entity during their séance.

We did experience some of the lights turning themselves on and off, with no one in the area, which was caught on camcorder. This is one of the more common reports from the house, but we were unable to conclude whether this was of paranormal origin or due to faulty electrics. But, as with the security and Navy's reports of this happening on several occasions, we could confirm that human intervention was not responsible. Strangely, it was very difficult to capture a good photograph within this building over

the entire weekend, whether day or night all of my shots were uncharacteristically blurred, out of focus or displaying other anomalies. Sadly we did not encounter the eighteenth-century bearded sailor seen wandering the dockyard. Some report him to be humming and smiling, which has led to his nickname of 'the smiling sailor'. Also reported is an eighteenth-century naval officer, observed staring out of a top-floor window, and a lady in a splendid cream dress gliding around the main bedroom. Perhaps the saddest accounts are the repeated sightings, and sometimes interaction with, a Victorian girl

The front of the Ropemaker's House.
(Courtesy of Stuart Andrews)

aged between five and ten playing with a doll, and of another six-year-old girl playing with a toy box. Both seem to haunt the upper floors, especially the third.

Night 2 – The Execution Cell and Ropery

It is fair to say there was a great deal of anticipation felt by the team as we entered the Hanging Cell for the first time; the range of reports and words of caution from the other team prepared us for what might be a very active night. Even the archway through the main building, which led down to the Dissection Room below, had a gloomy, almost oppressive atmosphere to it, made all the more so by the stark shades of the granite-facing blocks. While entering the Dissection Room, what appears to be an old mortuary table greets you, along with a now bricked-up alcove behind, it's said to have been used to shoot prisoners, should the noose not readily complete its macabre work. We were told by the Base Commander that military police had recently reported loud banging sounds coming from within the locked and empty rooms. Other reports include a bubbling reaction from a nearby covered area during heavy rain in the 1960s, presumed to be the burial pit where the recently executed were unceremoniously buried with a covering of quicklime.

Our expectations were sadly not met, and the time passed without incident, beside some technical difficulties and equipment failure. Although many believe such events accompany haunting experiences, this has to remain anecdotal, with coincidence a factor that cannot be ruled out. We were not fortunate enough to experience this or any of the other reported phenomena, which includes the ghosts of a twentieth-century suicide by hanging, and that of a murder victim in a nearby former latrine – his fate decided by others due to his alleged homosexuality. On reflection, this might have originated as a warning to sailors to avoid the temptation of such pursuits – we have also encountered a similar account from the North Caponier at Coalhouse Fort in Essex. If not urban legend or naval lore, then it is truly disturbing to think of two similarly concealed accounts, and how often this might have occurred elsewhere, possibly omitted from official records.

I then joined some of the base personnel and members of the other team for a walk around the South Yard. There was so much ground to cover I left the main team, including Becky, keeping a silent observational vigil of both the Hanging Cell and Dissection Room. Neither I nor the naval staff encountered anything unusual, but one of the mediums felt a sensation of being pushed backwards whilst walking down to a linking tunnel. There was a strong wind blowing up another tunnel, which links the existing Ropery and the site of the bomb-destroyed Ropery. Further research since leads me to conclude that this would be the wind flowing over the wall and then sinking to the base of the wall and being drawn up the tunnel. It was very interesting to see the full site of both the existing Ropery and its bombed-out sister building from the other side. I was able to gain a vivid impression of what they both would have previously looked like during their heyday.

At 1.30 p.m. the next vigil began in the Hangman's Cell. Various experiments and techniques were employed, including singing and talking in French. These sadly produced no results, except for a few anomalies on the night shot camcorders and digital cameras, including a previously captured image of a dark face which appeared on the floor inside the Ropery. Attempts to recreate this were successful and clearly due to a natural pattern

The rear of the Hanging Cell, Royal William Yard. (Courtesy of Stuart Andrews)

within the floor. Otherwise known as Pareidolia, the human mind will try and match what the eyes report to the brain with known associations; the human face is one of the most common, as recognising those of our parents is the first we learn as young children. Unfortunately nothing further was picked up by any of the team and this session was terminated at approximately 2.30 p.m. After a rest session, we moved back into the Ropery, while the other team focussed on the areas of the Ropemaker's House, which they were finding to be most active. According to Nancy Hammonds' *Ghosts of Plymouth*, a man wearing belt and braces over an unjacketed shirt has been seen here. Sadly, we did not encounter any such apparition, but I must say that this was the one area of the base where I felt distinctly unwelcome, as if we were being watched and our presence was strongly disapproved of. Perhaps this was due to it being such a cavernous area, but this was certainly in stark contrast to the Hanging Cell, despite the latter's preserved state.

After the Investigation

At 4.45 p.m. it was decided to call it a night, however, while walking back to the Ropemaker's House a couple of us heard a loud, heavy dragging sound coming from the area of the Hangman's Cell. Slightly nervous and alone, I walked around the corner to find the cause of this sound: traffic barriers being moved around by the Base Commander. In fact I gave him more of a fright, as he did not hear me walk up behind him!

The results showed that the psychic team experienced significantly more activity at both locations during both nights. This supports the idea that those with perceived psychic ability report a greater number of paranormal events. Whether this is due to their abilities, or their often firm beliefs priming them to expect such encounters, therefore finding them, is an unanswered question for the reader to consider. Subsequent enquires with the base revealed that a follow-up investigation was carried out by the medium-orientated team a few months later, details of which were never publicised. However, it is understood that the levels of reported experiences within the base have quietened down since, with no further accounts available from between the initial investigation and the present day. Despite the lack of any hard evidence gained during the weekend (after all, two nights is quite a short time to expect to experience a haunting), this was a truly unique investigation which raised many questions.

Could it be that the spirits at Devonport only wish to make themselves known to those they feel an affinity with, or a hatred for? A large number of the sightings and encounters have been reported by Naval and security personnel; it was also a police worker from the psychic team who had the most harrowing encounter, suffering a perceived psychic attack inside the Hanging Cell on the first night. It takes a certain type of person with strong nerves and self-confidence to patrol alone in the middle of the night, not the sort prone to flights of fancy or hallucinations or, indeed, a general fear of the dark or the unknown. Any such encounters are usually reported independently and are confined to one or two sites, and even certain areas within. The same is true of the experiences reported within the Naval Base; they are always in the same specific areas or buildings.

I'd like to wish Commander Crichton a happy retirement and also success for the Navy in realising their visitor centre project, and to thank them again for their hospitality. If anyone has any further accounts from Devonport, we would love to hear them through our website: info@hauntedplymouth.com info@supernaturalinvestigations.org.uk

Ferry House Inn

A 300-year-old inn, located in the picturesque area of Saltash Passage, was once used as a 'chop stop', where travellers could stop to enjoy a hot meal and sometimes a well-earned

Saltash Passage, showing the Royal Albert Bridge and Tamar Bridge.

Saltash Passage. (Courtesy of Derek Tait)

rest before continuing on their journey. The old Plymouth to Saltash ferry once ran daily from here, hence the inn's given name.

Back in 1993, the then new landlord and lady of the Ferry House Inn experienced first hand a couple of regulars from the spirit world. After being informed by some of the pub's regulars that the building was haunted by the restless ghosts of a young girl and an elderly woman, it was only a matter of time before the new owners 'met' the two shades dwelling within the building's ancient walls.

One evening, heavy, ponderous footsteps were heard upon the stairs that connect the two bars, even though no one was walking in this area at the time; this was followed by an instant drop in temperature. The owners' dog leapt forward, its lips curled back, heckles up and teeth exposed, barking and snarling at an area occupied by some unseen presence.

It is believed that the old lady who haunts this building once resided at the property and has some unfinished business, although it is not clear who the young girl is and why she still haunts the public house.

I have been told that the building is very atmospheric and that strange sounds are still being heard today by regulars at the Ferry House Inn.

Freedom Fields

The place name Freedom Fields can be traced back to 3 December 1643, when, upon this site, a fierce battle was fought during the English Civil War. The blood-soaked battlefield was to be remembered as Plymouth's greatest day in the English Civil War, and from this

Freedom Fields Park, site of the battlefield during the English Civil War.

Freedom Fields Park entrance.

day on, 3 December was to be remembered as the Sabbath Day Fight this was due to the town of Plymouth successfully fighting off an aggressive attack from Prince Maurice and his battle-hardened troops. The battle site is commemorated with the memorial plaque which can be seen in Freedom Fields Park.

The area just beyond the park is where the Plymouth workhouse once stood. Opened in 1858, the site grew over the years until it became home to the Greenbank Infirmary in 1909. In 1930 the workhouse system ceased and the whole site became the new Plymouth City Hospital. Due to its location upon high ground, the hospital was an easy target for enemy bombers during the Second World War. On the night of 13/14 January 1941, both wards 6 and 7 were completely destroyed by an enemy raid over the city. On 20 March 1941, another air raid over the city resulted in the brand new maternity unit at the hospital taking a direct hit. In the blast, fourteen newborn babies and three nurses were tragically killed.

Right & below: *All that remains of Greenbank Infirmary.*

Freedom Fields, Plymouth, one of the last remaining buildings from the hospital site.

In 1951, with the inauguration of the National Health Service, Plymouth City Hospital was renamed Freedom Fields Hospital. It was the birthplace to many generations of Plymothians, including this author, before it was closed in 1998.

There are a number of haunting tales associated with Freedom Fields Hospital; one particular account refers to Ward 13. The nurses on this ward had to put up with a poltergeist which did not have a calming bedside manner – turning lights on and off, slamming doors shut and, on a number of occasions, an invisible force physically pushed staff, which left a number of the nursing team quite shocked. This story made the local press, although when a newspaper reporter attended the ward hoping to experience the nebulous spirit for himself, he was left disappointed as the poltergeist went into hiding.

Harewood House

Harewood House, Plympton, was once the haunt of an elderly gentleman, who was described as wearing a red waistcoat and brown trousers. The first sighting of this restless spirit can be traced back to the winter of 1951 and, over the years, the house has been home to much reported paranormal activity, including heavy doors slamming shut and lights turning on and off, as if some invisible force was responsible. The most impressive tale involved the manifestation of the male spirit, which was witnessed first hand by a barman in the cellar of the old house.

Another documented account involved a framed picture placed on a wall, which was frequently found lying upon the floor as if removed from its secure fixing by an unseen force. The picture would be repositioned and, within a number of hours, would once again be found on the floor. All supernatural phenomena here ceased in November 1982, after a local priest was called to Harewood House to perform a blessing.

Unfortunately, Harewood House was destroyed by fire in 1985. A new house was constructed, although without many of the facilities the original building had.

Heart Radio, Plymouth

Patricia Duff recently contacted me as she had been experiencing some unusual happenings at her place of work, which happened to be none other than the home of Heart Radio Station, previously the headquarters of the independent radio station Plymouth Sound.

The studios are built upon the site of an old chapel, which is believed to account for the ghost of a little old lady who has appeared to a number of witnesses here in previous years. Therefore I was most intrigued to be contacted by Patricia with regard to her personal experiences, which took place in late 2009. I took the liberty of requesting Patricia to complete a witness interview form detailing exactly what she had witnessed and so forth. The following is a series of extracts from Patricia's interview form.

1. Where did you first experience the ghost(s) or phenomena?(Please indicate date, time of day and location)
On two separate occasions, the last occasion was on Tuesday, 1 December 2009 in the sales office. On both occasions it was dark and after 5 p.m. I was sat in the sales office with several members of staff.

2. Did your companion(s), if any, experience the phenomenon in any way?
On the second occasion the direction in which the lady went left a very cold area beside my Managing Director for some time afterwards.

3. If you experienced the phenomenon on more than one occasion, did it behave in the same way each time?
On the first occasion the lady went into the cupboard behind me, on the second she came out of the same cupboard.

4. If your experience was a sighting, please describe the manner in which it appeared and disappeared?
I only saw her reflection in the window but it was very clear, she seemed to just glide across behind me.

5. Were you expecting to have a paranormal experience at the location concerned?
No I was not expecting this; I was working away on my computer.

6. If your experience was a sighting, please describe the lighting conditions at the time.

It was dark outside, so the reflection in the window is crystal clear. I thought someone was passing the window the first time, then realised there was a 50 foot drop on the other side. Our office is well lit.

7. If your experience was aural (sounds), please describe it in detail, giving any comments on any strange or unusual elements of the noise.

There were no noises whatsoever, but the second time I saw her a really strange feeling came over me and I was covered in goose pimples.

8. If a sighting occurred, did it appear to be solid or translucent?

Solid.

9. If a sighting occurred, did it appear in colour, black and white or negative?

Colour. She was dressed in a beige and brown long dress/coat.

10. How did you feel during and after the experience(s): frightened; sad, glad, puzzled or some other emotion? If you felt frightened and had more than one experience of the same kind, did you feel more or less frightened on the subsequent occasions?

The first time I felt really calm, almost happy at seeing her, but the second time I felt a strange feeling as stated before – goose pimples and uneasy.

11. Did the ghost's movement seem natural or unnatural?

Very natural.

12. Did you notice anything else unusual at the time, such as sudden and intense silence, unusual sounds or scents? If so, exactly what did you notice?

Only the coldness of the direction she went into.

13. Did you feel any variation in temperature before or after you saw the sighting or heard the voice or while it was present? If so, please describe it.

The cold patch was approximately 6 foot from me and stayed there for about 15 minutes, others felt this too.

Mannamead Supernatural Investigations (UK) – Private House Investigation

It was a crisp winter's evening in late January 2008 – I had just knocked upon the door of a private dwelling in the Mannamead area of Plymouth. Patiently, I and several members of the Supernatural Investigations (UK) team waited to step forward over the threshold of this old Victorian house. The reason for our call was to undertake a paranormal investigation, with the intention of uncovering the truth behind the bizarre events that had unfolded prior to us arriving. The Supernatural Investigations (UK) team and I were about to come face-to-face with the realm of the supernatural.

The events leading up to this moment began with a voicemail left on my phone in early January 2008. An anxious female acquaintance of mine contacted me to ask for some assistance. For the purpose of confidentiality, I will refer to my friend as Mary.

Mary was aware of my interest in the paranormal and knew that during my free time I was a member of the paranormal group Supernatural Investigations (UK). It was because of this that Mary had contacted me and asked if I would consider undertaking a full investigation at her relatives' home in Mannamead. She explained that two close male relatives had both encountered what they described as

An old Plymouth door.

paranormal activity; this included a number of full-blown apparition sightings of a young girl, the movement of objects such as doors, along with a feeling of pure dread and of not being alone in certain areas of the property. The activity had been occurring throughout the building for several months, although in late 2007 it had reached a whole new level, with one of Mary's young relatives being left so shocked by a particularly frightening experience that he was no longer happy to stay at the property. It was at this point that Mary decided to seek advice and the possibility of an investigation to uncover who or what was responsible for the mysterious happenings at the building.

I would like to point out that Supernatural Investigations (UK) is an experienced team of serious paranormal researchers which adopts both a scientific and psychic approach. The team has participated in and arranged dozens of paranormal investigations for over eleven years, including organising and hosting public charity ghost nights. Our focus is on serious investigative work at a variety of venues, from private houses, hotels and pubs to outdoor sites, castles and historical properties.

The Investigation

After introductions and a full tour of the property, the Supernatural Investigations (UK) team set up all the relevant equipment required to hopefully capture any paranormal activity during our time spent at this location.

As team leader, I divided the investigation team into two smaller teams, which comprised of each individual investigator being given a set role/task to undertake during the investigation. No one on the team, other than myself, had prior knowledge of the case file, thus ruling out potential autosuggestion that may have arisen from anyone knowing about the site.

I have included below a brief summary of one of our psychic's findings, which was submitted to be included in the final investigation report. I have chosen this purely because the information gathered by the team's psychic tied in with actual prior events and activity that had been witnessed by the home owners and other relatives.

On arrival at the house at 20:30, I went via the front room to the dining room and immediately sensed a presence in the archway between the two rooms. This was a male, around forty years old, tall, and slim, with dark hair and a beard.

During the first séance, I sensed this spirit was called Graham. He felt connected in some way to the home owner and may possibly have worn glasses. He had brown cords on. I was also aware of a male spirit in the doorway behind Stuart (investigator), who appeared only as a black shadow.

On the walk around I felt most areas of the house were calm until I reached the second flight of stairs. Immediately I saw a young female on the third stair down from the top. I was very anxious in her presence and felt my solar plexus doing somersaults. She had her face covered with a white, thin cloth and was wearing an old-fashioned, white cotton nightdress. Her hair was long and straggly, which looked like it could be a dirty blond colour, and she drew my attention to the fact that she had bare feet. (In fact she showed me her feet several times throughout the night.) She also made me aware that she had taken her own life through hanging herself from a beam above one of the attic bedrooms. Other than this she did not communicate anything else to me at this stage. She felt very intimidating!

In the kitchen I was made aware of a gentleman who may have been a handyman here at one time and a lady who seemed to be a past owner. The gentleman was wearing a flatcap, black Wellington boots and a blue jacket. The lady had an apron on and was cooking. As he came in they said 'hello' and went about their business, oblivious to us. I believe this was just a replay of a happy past event in the house and the whole scene had a good feeling about it.

During group A's time in the dining room, at approximately 22:00, I popped into the lounge to collect my notebook. I couldn't help but feel that I was being watched through the front room door, which was slightly ajar. I watched and waited for a few moments but the door didn't move, although I really felt as though it was going to, it was a really odd sensation.

While our group were in the child's bedroom on the first floor, I sensed the girl in white by the door looking in at us. However, she would not come into the room. Other than this I didn't feel anything in this room, it all seemed calm.

I then tried some psycometary; by doing this I picked up on the memory of a gentleman in a black suit with long tails and a high-collared shirt. He was very angry and was beating a woman with a stick, who was wearing a long, full-skirted dress.

They looked as though they were husband and wife and could have been Victorian. It wasn't very pleasant to see, but like the scene in the kitchen, it was just a memory of a past occurrence in the house and they were totally unaware of me.

The group agreed that I and another lady should go up to the attic by ourselves, but when I got to the foot of the stairs I felt I couldn't go up any further. I waited by the door of the boy's room and I knew that the girl in white was with me. I tried to link in with her, but she wouldn't communicate with me. Suddenly I felt a tightening sensation around my neck, especially between the Adam's apple and the tops of my collarbones. This was quite frightening and the pressure made me physically gag. I stepped back into the boy's room and the sensation lifted. I know Jason (investigator) was filming in the room at the time so I hope this was caught on camera. I am positive that the girl was putting this sensation upon me.

Later in the girl's room in the attic, I sensed a little girl of seven or eight years of age, wearing an old-fashioned school uniform. She seemed quite happy and is aware of the girl who lives in the house. She may have even shown herself to her. She has a bubbly personality and likes to play jokes on people. I was also made aware of the girl in white standing outside the door. I noted that this spirit had a thing for doors, but I couldn't work out why.

The group then split into two, with the males of the group going into the other attic room. Whilst it was just me and the three ladies in this room, I began to feel a rocking sensation as the girl in white began connecting with me. I was sitting on a chair and was physically rocking backwards and forwards, involuntarily. I could see the girl in white sitting on a cold, bare floor hugging her knees, also rocking. She told me she had a name beginning with S, which felt very much like Sarah. Then she showed me that she had been locked in and left to starve in one of the attic rooms. She was really angry and gave me the sense that she may have gone mad in here, or suffered with mental health problems because of it. She again showed me her feet, but this time they were dangling out of the bottom of her nightdress as though she'd been hung.

After this vigil, I was stood on the first floor landing by the toilet speaking with the same three ladies, when again Sarah came to me and showed me that the man I had seen earlier in the boy's room had been the one who had beaten her, put her in the attic and starved her. She was really aggressive when showing me this and kept repeating the words 'the bastard'. As a result of this she took her own life and has not properly passed over. She lingers here looking for him and hates it when the doors are closed in the house. I believe she is responsible for pushing doors open and for locking the attic doors. She has also appeared to the males in the house in order to frighten them. It was interesting to note that she would only communicate with me when there were no males around. I suggested that the teams split into male and female teams, as I was sure the males would get a reaction from her, which they did.

For me, the rest of the evening was quiet and I didn't encounter the girl again after this. I did feel the atmosphere lift after she had managed to tell me why she was here.

I can confirm that the males on the investigation team did indeed encounter an array of unusual activity at this location, particularly in the attic rooms. This included loud taps and bangs, along with some very significant readings that were picked up using a selection of EVP (Electronic Voice Phenomenon) equipment and temperature readings, not to mention a selection of interesting readings with the EMF (Electromagnetic Field) meters in certain parts of the property.

I can conclude by saying that since our investigation in January 2008, the activity at this location has ceased. Could this be a result of the restless spirits being acknowledged?

Molesworth Road

The old parish church in Stoke Dameral, which dates back several hundred years, stands upon the crest of a hill which overlooks a narrow valley. This church is the centrepiece to a remarkable supernatural tale which links the past with the present.

A gentleman named John once lived in a property located on Molesworth Road in Plymouth. The Victorian house that John called home was only a short walk from Stoke Dameral church. Back in the eighteenth century, the area where John's house was situated would have been open scrubland, and Molesworth Road back then would have just been an old stone track.

One April evening, John was at his home in Molesworth Road when he entered his kitchen and was suddenly greeted with a very strong smell of fresh fish, a most distinctive odour. He didn't think much of it until the same smell returned the following evening. It was most bizarre, as the phantom smell occurred at exactly the same time of day, which was around 5 p.m. The next evening the same thing happened, and again the following evening and so forth.

One particular weekend John was staying away from home and asked his neighbour to check on his property, which his neighbour was more than happy to do, although upon entering John's home his neighbour also detected the strong smell of fish.

It is believed that there is a link between smells and the paranormal. When you talk about hauntings, people presume that you are referring to ghostly sightings of shadowy figures. However, this is not always the case, for odours are also associated with the paranormal. For example, you may smell the strong scent of a woman's perfume in a haunted location, or maybe the distinctive odour of pipe tobacco, even though at the time it may be evident that no one is smoking. Then, within a split second, the smell dissipates as quickly as it manifested.

Back to the ghostly tale, where, at this point, John had decided that enough was enough and sought assistance in finding who, or what, was responsible for the prevalent smell of fresh fish in his home. He was given the name of a gentleman named Peter – a psychic medium.

Peter met up with John at his home in Molesworth Road; the medium had no prior knowledge of the activity that had been witnessed by John and at least six other separate individuals.

Peter wasted no time in describing who was responsible for the elusive smell. The phantom was described as around sixty years of age, short and stocky with a thick, grey beard. The date given to Peter was 1759 and the male presence also revealed his name as being James Goldsworthy. James had been a local fish merchant. The spirit continued to

Two views of Molesworth Road, Plymouth.

communicate with the medium and explained that his daily routine involved travelling from his home located close to the Barbican, from where he would collect and sell fish to other areas of Plymouth and the outskirts of the town. His actual route took him across the scrubland – directly through what was now John's home. The spirit continued to converse with Peter and explained that he was beaten and robbed in the area where John's kitchen was located. The savage attack left the fish merchant with a broken arm, which in turn resulted in a string of bad luck.

The reason, therefore, why the spirit continued to haunt this location was because in life it was where he had endured a brutal attack which had been the catalyst to his misfortune.

The medium felt it necessary to assist with passing the spirit on to the other side, to be united with his family. In what was quite an emotional task, Peter worked with the restless soul and eventually crossed him over.

John was so intrigued by the event that he decided to try and find out more information on James Goldsworthy. Local burial records revealed that James Goldsworthy was indeed a real person. The 7th of November 1774 refers to a burial of one James Goldsworthy.

I had the pleasure of meeting John one cold, autumn night at the Foxhound Inn at Brixton, near Plymouth. He confirmed for me that all the events that occurred when he resided at Molesworth Road were 100 per cent genuine, which leads me to believe that this is a true account of a ghost from the past making contact with the living of today.

The Morley Arms

Located on the well-travelled Billacombe Road, the Morley Arms' rear garden backs onto the mouth of the river Plym. This building was constructed in 1762 by the architect Meadows Rendell, originally built to form part of the vast Saltram estate, owned at the time by Lord Morley.

Quarry workers and travellers alike would have frequented the inn in bygone days, which was also popular with individuals travelling along one of the main coaching routes to and from Plymouth. At the rear of the property is what remains of a number of stone mooring posts, which were once used to shore-up sailing ships. Bearing this in mind, the venue would have proved a perfect location for press gangs preying on unsuspecting customers passing through the Morley Arms.

I received the following email from a previous member of staff regarding the spirits that dwell in this old inn:

Whilst at the Morley Arms in Plymstock I experienced several unusual happenings. While alone in the pub (before opening time, with just the chef and the cleaner present) I saw a young girl run from the direction of the lounge through to the bar and then out into the rear gardens, even though at the time there were no young girls around the location at all!

Another occurrence happened after the kitchen had closed and I was left alone cleaning up as the chef had finished for the day. One of the waitresses was clearing the tables in the bar area when something slammed quite firmly into my shoulder. It felt like a hand. I turned around instantly but there was no sign of anyone there. I immediately went out to the bar to ask who the joker was, but the waitress did not know what I was talking about.

It is said that the ghost of lady stands at the bar. One of the bar staff actually went to serve this woman, which completely confused the two gentlemen standing at the bar on either side of the lady, who couldn't see her.

On a final note, I too have visited this fascinating inn on a number of occasions and can honestly say that at times you can detect a certain atmosphere, although to date I have not come face-to-face with any of the Morley's sprits.

Mount Gould Hospital

The original site of Mount Gould Hospital was acquired by Plymouth Borough Council in January 1885. Upon this 20-acre site, numerous wooden buildings were erected for an infectious diseases hospital. In 1889 the Infectious Diseases Act became law and it was apparent that the current wooden structures were not up to specification. Therefore a more solid structure was designed and built to replace them. Over the last 100 years the site of Mount Gould Hospital has changed quite dramatically, with modern buildings replacing older ones.

Certain areas of Mount Gould Hospital are reputedly built upon the site of an ancient battlefield. Over the years, hospital staff have experienced strange disturbances of varying intensity, ranging from unearthly sounds, including groans emanating from a specific area that is quite clearly vacant.

The most common sighting witnessed by a number of individuals is that of a Lady in White. On one particular evening, a male member of staff witnessed the phantom glide into a room occupied by a patient. Upon further inspection the room was found to be empty, with the exception of the male patient, who was sound asleep. In a mysterious twist, the male patient unexpectedly passed away before dawn the next morning, even though he had been in a stable condition and was not being treated for a life-threatening condition.

Old Road Inn

In August 1992 it was reported in the *Evening Herald* that this public house on Old Laira Road was being haunted by a very helpful ghost. The mysterious presence had been felt around the main bar area and had a habit of emptying the rubbish bin from behind the bar. The landlord stated that one moment the bin would be almost full to overflowing and the next it would be completely empty, its contents vanished into thin air.

Plympton Megabowl

In 2007, staff working at the Plympton Megabowl sought assistance from a local spiritualist medium following an increase in poltergeist activity and eyewitness accounts of unearthly figures at the site. It was believed that the activity was related to the original building previously located on the site. This gives weight to the possibility that in some circumstances the spirits of the dead are connected to the land rather than the current structures.

Widey Court

Widey Court was situated in the parish of Eggbuckland. Widey's roots can be traced back to 1590/91, when Sir Francis Drake constructed two mills in the area. The mills' purpose was to connect to Drake's brand new leat system, which originates on Dartmoor.

In December 1643, during the English Civil War, Prince Maurice based his headquarters for a short time at Widey House.

Widey House earned the right to be named a 'Court' when King Charles I held court here during the Civil War. At the time it was owned by Yeoman Heale, a farmer and staunch Royalist. It was from here that King Charles demanded the surrender of Plymouth.

The King resided at Widey House from the 9th to the 14th of September 1644. It is said that after the monarch's stay, neither of his rooms were used or even disturbed for many years.

The house was rebuilt between 1675 and 1699, with a number of alterations in the eighteenth century. The Morshead family owned Widey House for over 300 years, ownership later passing to two naval gentlemen who intended to turn the ancient manor house into a high class hotel, although this failed to happen.

In its heyday, Widey Court consisted of an inner and outer hall, two conservatories, dining room, morning room, a library, billiard room, cloakroom, lavatory, two staircases – consisting of a main staircase and a secondary flight – servants' hall, scullery, pantry, kitchen, and store room. The house had two further vast cellars in the basement. The first floor had a total of eight bedrooms, along with three dressing dooms and two nurseries. On the attic floor another eight bedrooms were situated along with a box room. The grounds also housed stables, a coach house and a dairy.

Widey was requisitioned in 1941 and used by Plymouth City Police until 1945, but, after years of neglect, the house was eventually demolished in 1954. Today, Widey Court Primary School sits upon the site where the impressive manor house once stood.

Widey's Haunted Past

Widey had all the ingredients of a classic haunted manor house, including priest holes, secret tunnels and passages.

The ghost of a Lady in White is one of the well-known phantoms to have haunted the building. Lieutenant-Colonel H. W. Markwick tried to save Widey Court from going to rack and ruin in the early 1950s and spent a large amount of his time wandering around the manor, although he never encountered the Lady in White himself.

However, two unfortunate individuals did not escape an encounter with the ghost. The married couple had been working on the estate in 1952 when the Lady in White appeared before them. This was such a heart-stopping experience that the woman's husband was almost frightened to death. The source of these hauntings was thought to date back to a brutal murder at the house. One of the daughters from the manor house was apparently murdered on her own wedding night by one of the house's butlers. The butler was so distraught by the impending marriage, as, unbeknown to her, he had secretly loved the bride for many years, that in a fit of jealous rage he killed the woman he loved rather than see her married to another man.

Another phantom sighting is said to have taken place in 1873, when an impressive dinner party took place at Widey Court House.

On the way home in her carriage after the evening's party, one particular dinner guest, an elderly lady, commented upon the rude man who had sat next to her during the evening meal, without speaking a single word to her. She recalled that he was wearing a very unusual uniform, like that of a solider from the English Civil War era. It was at this point that the elderly lady was informed that there had been no one sitting next to her throughout the evening meal. That particular place had not been occupied due to the guest being unable to attend and the seat was therefore vacant.

Could this phantom dinner guest have been one of King Charles' officers, sitting in stony silence next to the woman?

Radford House

Tales of lost treasure and secret tunnels – what more could you ask for from a classic haunting dating back many centuries?

After almost 600 years, Radford House, which was known to have played a major part in shaping Plymouth's history, was sadly demolished in 1937.

The land where the old house once stood was originally owned by William Le Abbé during the reign of King Henry III (1216-1272). The successor to William was to be Walter Le Abbé, who took the name Radford.

At least two Norman abbeys were situated upon the vast amount of land that was passed on to Walter. The Radfords continued to hold the land until it passed over to the Harris family during the reign of Edward IV (1461-1483).

Radford House was originally built in what was commonly known as an Elizabethan E-plan house.

During the reign of Queen Elizabeth I, Sir Christopher Harris resided at Radford House. He also represented the town of Plymouth in Parliament. Sir Christopher Harris was a naval man and held the rank of Vice Admiral of Devon. This gentleman would once have stood shoulder-to-shoulder with a number of well-known names, including Sir Francis Drake and Sir Walter Raleigh. Thus it is quite possible that England's finest sea captains and admirals would have frequented Radford House.

One of the legends of lost treasure is associated with the Harris family. No fewer than twenty-two silver dishes with the Harris family crest engraved upon them were presented to Sir Christopher Harris between 1581 and 1602 as a memorial to his success as an Admiral during the Anglo-Spanish War (1585-1604). However, during a rushed act to prevent the silver being taken by Parliamentary forces during the English Civil War (1641-1651), it was hidden upon Dartmoor, where it laid in its shallow, earthy grave for over 200 years.

Unfortunately, the Harris family were unable to relocate the buried silver, that was until a farm labourer working upon Dartmoor unearthed the Harris family silver in 1827.

Sir Walter Raleigh was imprisoned at Radford House in June 1618 for ten days after being arrested upon his return to England empty handed, following his disastrous expedition to El Dorado in search of the gold King James I desperately anticipated him finding. Raleigh was transported to the Tower of London, where he awaited trial for numerous charges, including high treason. On 29 October 1618, Raleigh was executed at Whitehall. It is said that his headless body was buried, but his devoted wife continued to carry Raleigh's severed head in a large bag everywhere she went until the day she died.

Over the years the house underwent a number of major alterations, with the addition of several new wings, along with other Georgian façades. The building now boasted fifty rooms, making it one of the largest houses in the local area and on a par with the impressive Lanhydrock House in Cornwall.

Radford has its fair share of phantoms, which also haunt the wooded valley near Radford Lake. Radford Lake is divided by a narrow causeway. Upon the opposite side of the boundary is Hooe Lake, which is a tidal lake.

The causeway at Hooe Lake.

A fearless phantom monk has been witnessed close by the gates en route to the old chapel-at-east, although those who have seen him all state that they could not make out his face due to the fact it is hidden by the large hood on his habit.

The White Lady of Radford is probably the most well known of all the ghosts said to haunt this area, although there are several different ideas about who this phantom female is and where the haunting originates. The ghost is suspected to be a former resident of Radford House.

One legend has it that the lady in question secretly escaped from Radford House to meet up with a female acquaintance from a nearby village. She had been forbidden by her parents to meet with her friend as it was thought that she should not be mixing with anyone below her class.

The rendezvous was to end in disaster. Away from the safety of her home she headed straight towards Radford Lake, where she was united with her friend and they set out onto the lake in a small boat. In a moment of chaos, the young lady fell overboard and, unable to swim and being weighed down by the material of her heavy white dress, she slipped into the dark waters of Radford Lake and to her watery grave.

Radford Lake, where the White Lady is said to haunt.

The fable does not end here, as the phantom of the Lady in White has been spotted sitting upon the bank of the lake. It is also believed that she is the spectre seen wandering aimlessly around the grounds where the old Radford House once stood.

Site of the old boathouse at Radford Park.

Old building at Radford Lake.

Ancient ruin at Radford Lake.

Radford park lake.

White Lady Road.

The legend lives on today in White Lady Road, which has been named after the mysterious female ghost. This road can be found down towards Radford Dip, although if you dare to visit this road, be on your guard, as you may come face-to-face with this elegant spirit.

Royal William Yard

The Royal William Yard was designed by Sir John Rennie (1794–1878). Situated upon 16 acres, the Royal William Yard's main purpose was as a victualling (food and provisions) depot for the Royal Navy. Work commenced in 1826 with the construction being completed in 1835.

Upon entering the large granite archway, a 12ft-tall stone statue of King William IV towers above visitors from its impressive plateau. Located off to the right of the entrance was the old slaughterhouse and to the left-hand side stood the old police house. It is known that no fewer than 250 personnel were employed in the Yard at its peak.

In 1993 the Yard was closed and taken over by the Plymouth Development Corporation, and after several million pounds were spent on development, the Royal William Yard has been given a new lease of life, with many buildings being converted into luxury apartments.

In its glory days many tradespeople would have plied their trades behind the large stone walls that surrounded the perimeter of the Royal William Yard, including bakers, butchers and coopers. With such a fascinating history, it is of no surprise that fellow traders and service personnel held this area very dear to them in life and, for a small handful, in death too.

Paranormal sightings and sounds have been quite the norm here. Other supernatural activity has included noticeable temperature drops in certain areas of the Yard.

The Parade Ground once housed cattle awaiting their fate as Bully Beef. Sometimes, late in the evening, the eerie sound of cattle hooves stamping upon old cobblestones has been heard, even though this very area is today grassed over.

I have been given fresh information from a reliable source who, at the time of writing, is working at the Royal William Yard for a building contractor. It seems that paranormal activity there is still occurring even today. The latest accounts refer to January 2010.

In Residents 1, a tradesman heard the sound of someone moving upon the stairs. It sounded like a woman in a large dress (likened to the sound of a long flowing wedding dress). Upon immediate inspection, there was no sign of anyone being present.

Another odd occurrence is the sound of old parlour music in one particular area of Residents 1. Once again there is no obvious source for the phantom noise.

Old photograph of the Royal William Yard. (Courtesy of Derek Tait)

Right: *The gateway to the Royal William Yard, surmounted by Sir John Rennie's statue of King William IV. (Courtesy of John Van der Kiste)*

Below: *The former parade ground at the Royal William Yard, which has now been grassed over.*

Above: *The Melville Clock Tower, Royal William Yard.*

Left: *Residents 1 and 2 at the Royal William Yard.*

One gentleman had quite a shock as he was carrying out an inspection up a ladder at the rear of the old police house. His attention was drawn to a window, where he saw the shade of a man dressed in an old-fashioned police officer's uniform and sporting a handlebar moustache.

A woman on the first floor in Residents 2 witnessed a full-blown apparition of a man dressed in an old naval officer's uniform.

An oppressive feeling has been felt by a few individuals in the vicinity of the Melville Clock Tower.

The bakery and cooperage at the Royal William Yard.

I have also been informed recently that when building work was undertaken in the old mills and bakery within the past ten years, a number of spooky occurrences have happened. The heavy wooden doors located in this area, which were at the time coated with metal for fire protection, were known to open and shut on their own accord. I have been told that these doors are not easily moved due to their weight.

Tavistock Road

The following story featured on ITV's *This Morning* more than ten years ago. During a Halloween phone-in, presenters Richard and Judy asked viewers to contact them with their own genuine spooky tales. The show received numerous callers relating supernatural encounters on the A386 (known locally as Tavistock Road), including one from a local man.

It was early morning and the gentleman was travelling in his car on his way to work along the Tavistock Road. Midway through his journey he sighted a man and a woman just ahead of him on the other side of the road running hand-in-hand at quite some pace, as if they were fleeing someone or something. The driver drew closer to the couple and, just as he was about to pass them, the woman stumbled and fell directly into the driver's path. The driver braced himself for the inevitable impact, as it would have been impossible to have stopped in time to avoid hitting the young woman. He stamped on his brakes, fully

Tavistock Road.

expecting to feel his car hit the woman, but there was no such collision – no sound or feeling of impact. He immediately jumped out of his now stationary vehicle, expecting to find a gruesome scene before him, but was mystified to find no sign of the woman or her male companion. It was as if they had simply vanished into thin air without a trace.

I have personally travelled along this stretch of road many times, although to date have not witnessed the phantom couple first hand, but from the number of reported sightings it seems that they do indeed haunt this ancient stretch of highway that links Tavistock with Plymouth.

Afterword

I have been actively investigating the paranormal for the past ten years, and from a personal point of view can confirm that during my time spent at a wide array of haunted sites around Plymouth and beyond, I have indeed witnessed what I can only describe as first-hand paranormal activity.

The two most common questions that I have been asked whilst either carrying out a paranormal investigation or during one of my Plymouth ghost walks are, 'Do you believe in ghosts?' and 'Have you ever seen a one?' My reply to both questions is yes.

I hope that you have enjoyed your journey through the supernatural realm of Plymouth, I do recommend that if you have the opportunity to visit any of the locations mentioned in this book then please do so, but be warned – you may indeed come face-to-face with the shadier side of Plymouth.

Kevin Hynes, 2010

Sir Francis Drake's statue on Plymouth Hoe.

Bibliography & Further Reading

Books

Ash, R. et al., *Folklore, Myths and Legends of Britain* (Readers Digest Association Ltd, 1977)
Barber, S., Barber, C., *Haunted Pubs in Devon* (Obelisk Publications, 2004)
Brown, T., *Devon Ghosts* (Jarrold Colour Publications, 1982)
Chard, J., *Haunted Happenings in Devon* (Obelisk Publications, 1988)
Coates, G., *Plymouth Gin: The Adventure* (Coates & Co. Ltd, 2003)
Hammonds, N., *Ghosts of Plymouth* (Obelisk Publications, 1996)
Holgate, M., *Celebrity Ghosts of Devon* (Obelisk Publications, 2003)
Matthews, R., *Haunted Places of Devon* (Countryside Books, 2004)
Noble, S., *Plymouth's Barbican and Castle: An Historic Landscape and its Archaeology* (Sarum Graphics, 2000)
Underwood, P., *Ghosts of Devon* (Bossiney Books, 2003)
White, A., *Sir Francis Drake: Devon's Flawed Hero* (Bossiney Books, 2003)

Websites

www.paranormaldatabase.com (11/2009)
www.plymouthdata.info (06/2009)
www.ghostfinder.co.uk (07/2009)
www.hauntedplymouth.com
www.supernaturalinvestigations.org.uk